TEACHING
IN THE
FLAT WORLD

TEACHING IN THE FLAT WORLD

LEARNING FROM HIGH-PERFORMING SYSTEMS

Linda Darling-Hammond
Robert Rothman

with contributions by

Pasi Sahlberg, Barry Pervin, Carol Campbell, and Tan Lay Choo

TEACHERS COLLEGE PRESS

TEACHERS COLLEGE | COLUMBIA UNIVERSITY

NEW YORK AND LONDON

Published by Teachers College Press, 1234 Amsterdam Avenue, New York, NY 10027

World map courtesy of FreeVectormaps.com, under a creative commons attribution license.

Figures in Chapter 4 courtesy of Ontario Ministry of Education © 2013, 2015. Queen's Printer for Ontario. Reproduced with permission.

Figure in Chapter 5 courtesy of Academy of Singapore Teachers, Ministry of Education, Singapore. Reproduced with permission.

Library of Congress Cataloging-in-Publication Data

Darling-Hammond, Linda, 1951–
    Teaching in the flat world : learning from high-performing systems / Linda Darling-Hammond, Robert Rothman ; with contributions by Pasi Sahlberg, Barry Pervin, Carol Campbell, and Tan Lay Choo.
    pages cm
    Includes bibliographical references and index.
    ISBN 978-0-8077-5647-8 (pbk.)—ISBN 978-0-8077-5648-5 (hardcover)—ISBN 978-0-8077-7375-8 (ebook)
    1. Effective teaching—Cross-cultural studies. 2. Teacher effectiveness—Cross-cultural studies. 3. Teaching—Standards—Cross-cultural studies. 4. Teachers—Training of—Cross-cultural studies. 5. Teachers—Recruiting—Cross-cultural studies. 6. Educational evaluation—Cross-cultural studies. I. Rothman, Robert, 1959– II. Title.
    LB1025.3.D37 2015
    371.102—dc23

                  2014049334

ISBN 978-0-8077-5647-8 (paper)
ISBN 978-0-8077-5648-5 (hardcover)
ISBN 978-0-8077-7375-8 (ebook)

Printed on acid-free paper
Manufactured in the United States of America

22   21   20   19   18   17   16   15   8   7   6   5   4   3   2   1

Contents

Acknowledgments

This book grew out of a symposium held in September 2010 in Washington, DC, that was sponsored by the Alliance for Excellent Education and the Stanford Center for Opportunity Policy in Education (SCOPE) and funded by the Education Funders Strategy Group (EFSG). The editors would like to thank Bob Wise, president of the Alliance, and Dan Leeds and Terri Shuck of EFSG for their support.

The editors would also like to thank the authors, Carol Campbell, Barry Pervin, Pasi Sahlberg, and Tan Lay Choo, who participated in the symposium and provided a great deal of insight about teacher and school leader policies in their respective nations.

An earlier version of some of these chapters was issued as a report released by the Alliance and SCOPE. The editors would like to thank Kate Bradley for her editing of that report.

TEACHING
IN THE
FLAT WORLD

CHAPTER 1

Developing Effective Teaching
Why Search Globally?

Linda Darling-Hammond
Robert Rothman

In the United States, teacher quality has clearly risen to the top of the education policy agenda. At the start of the Obama administration, the U.S. Department of Education identified the issue as one of four key elements in its Race to the Top competition, which allocated $4 billion to states that adopted specific policies and proposed strategies for implementing them. Since then, the department and major philanthropies have developed an aggressive agenda around "teacher effectiveness," and more than 30 states, responding to Race to the Top and other federal incentives, adopted laws revamping teacher education and evaluation systems, hoping to ensure that teachers are successful in the classroom.

While educators and policymakers generally agree that enabling teachers to improve student learning is one of the most significant ways to raise student achievement, there are heated disagreements about the most useful ways to do this. The conviction that teachers are important is backed up by research. The evidence is clear that teaching is one of the most important school-related factors in student achievement (National Commission on Teaching and America's Future [NCTAF], 1996, 1997; Clotfelter, Ladd, & Vigdor, 2007), and improving teachers' capacities to teach all students well can raise overall student achievement levels (Darling-Hammond, Wei, Andree, Richardson, & Orphanos, 2009; Yoon, Duncan, Lee, Scarloss, & Shapley, 2007).

The evidence base for the wide-ranging policy proposals for improving teacher effectiveness, however, is less clear. Some proposals have been studied—certain teacher preparation designs, induction and professional development approaches, specific evaluation strategies, and compensation reforms. And some—though certainly not all—findings are consistent across studies. At the same time, particular policies are only useful if, together, they result in talented people wanting to become educators, having effective pathways to allow them to do so, and working in contexts that help them become and remain effective, and continue to learn and improve. These outcomes can only result from a system in which all the components work together to produce the overarching goal of a consistently well-prepared educator workforce that can provide effective teaching for all students.

It does little good, for example, to develop a strategy that raises standards for teaching if there are insufficient incentives to attract enough individuals who can meet the standards. Similarly, if lowering the standards addresses the problem of shortages, but then the less-prepared entrants leave at high rates, creating churn and instability in the teaching force, the solution has merely created another problem. And if new evaluation systems weed out more teachers but meanwhile lower morale and chase good teachers away, districts may win the teacher evaluation battle, only to lose the quality teaching war.

EXAMINING SYSTEMS

For these reasons and others, we have chosen to examine how high-performing nations create coherent *systems* for developing consistently strong teaching. The countries featured in this volume have well-developed and effective systems for recruiting, preparing, developing, and retaining teachers and school leaders. Examining their efforts is valuable for a number of reasons:

- First, they broaden the view of what is possible. Too often, policymakers remain stuck with conventional ideas, bound by precedents in their own context, and are unable to see options that might be available and successful. By providing policymakers with an expanded view of the policy choices that might be available, comparisons can expand the toolbox.
- Second, international comparisons show how ideas work in practice at the system level. By exploring other systems in depth, policymakers can see what the implementation challenges are, how other nations dealt with them, and what remains to be solved. Such explorations

> Expanded policy choices can expand the toolbox.

can help enable policymakers to put in place new policies with a clearer eye.

For its examination of teacher effectiveness policies, we looked to Finland, Ontario (Canada), and Singapore. These jurisdictions have attracted a great deal of attention in U.S. education policy circles recently, and with good reason. Most significantly, they get good results: They are among the highest-performing jurisdictions in international tests of student achievement, and their results are among the most equitable in the world. The gaps between the lowest-performing and highest-performing students in Finland, Ontario, and Singapore are much smaller than in the United States, and the average performance is quite high (OECD, 2010b, 2013).

These jurisdictions also represent models that the United States can learn from. Although the nations are considerably smaller than the United States as a whole, they are equivalent in size to substantial U.S. states, where most education policy is made and takes effect. In terms of population, Finland is about the size of Colorado; Ontario is slightly larger than Illinois; and Singapore is about the size of Minnesota. This is especially relevant because, in the United States, education systems are operated by states, which have responsibility for virtually all of the key functions associated with developing a human capital system for schools.

In addition, the jurisdictions we examine are increasingly diverse in student population—some even more so than the typical American state. Finland, the most homogeneous, has recently attracted growing numbers of immigrants from the Middle East and Africa, and some schools in Helsinki serve a majority of immigrant students. Despite the fact that many immigrant families and youth arrive with much lower levels of education, these schools still show achievement levels that are similar to other schools'. About a fourth of Ontario's residents are from outside Canada, a ratio higher than most states in the United States. And Singapore has a number of minority groups speaking four official languages (and many more unofficial ones), representing the diverse communities that make up that nation-state.

> The jurisdictions we examine are increasingly diverse—some even more so than the typical American state.

Finland, Ontario, and Singapore also provide important lessons for discussions of policies to develop teacher and school leader effectiveness. All attribute their educational success in large measure to their efforts to recruit, prepare, develop, and retain a strong educator workforce within a purposeful human capital system.

EXAMINING POLICIES IN THE UNITED STATES

The fact that we look to other nations to provide lessons about how systems may be organized to accomplish effective teaching does not mean that there are not important lessons to learn from our own experience. Because of our 50-state federalist system and our traditions of local control, the United States has one of the most diverse education systems in the world. In almost every arena, there are highly effective policies, practices, and institutions that are the envy of others in the world, including the countries we examined, who study and emulate them.

In addition, there is more intensive research about the outcomes of these approaches in the United States than anywhere else. This means that we understand a great deal about what works under what circumstances—as well as what doesn't work—from which we and others can learn. We share these findings here as well, to set the context for cross-country learning.

THE ORGANIZATION OF THIS BOOK

In Chapter 2 of this volume we describe the diverse range of practices and policies regarding teachers and school leadership in the United States and some of what has been learned about the effects of many of them. We also examine recent reforms and their odds for improving teaching. We highlight elements of success, while we also illuminate the challenges of a policy landscape that changes frequently and is often not well aligned or coherent.

In Chapters 3–5 we examine, in turn, the systems for developing effective teachers and school leaders in Finland, Ontario, and Singapore, respectively. Each of these chapters is authored by one or more scholars from the relevant jurisdiction, with extensive knowledge of the history and current status of policy and practice in that system. The chapters treat questions of recruitment, preparation, induction, professional learning, and evaluation for teachers and school leaders.

We learn that while each has a systemic approach, each places somewhat different emphases on different aspects of the system: In Finland, preservice preparation for teachers is a linchpin that anchors the other components. In Ontario, innovative and widespread inservice development

> We understand a great deal about what works under what circumstances— as well as what doesn't work.

> While each [jurisdiction] has a systemic approach, each places somewhat different emphases.

performs this function; there is a special emphasis on preparing and supporting both teacher and administrative leaders. In Singapore, career development systems are a major centerpiece of the overall approach to effectiveness. These are like lenses of a prism that one looks through to illuminate the entire enterprise.

Finally, in Chapter 6 we draw common lessons from across these chapters, in hope that the entire picture comes into focus in ways that can be instructive to educators and policymakers from many distinctive contexts. We hope this book will be helpful to educators, policymakers, and researchers seeking strategies that can strengthen the teaching profession and ultimately help design systems that expand learning opportunities for all children.

CHAPTER 2

Teacher Quality Initiatives in the United States

Robert Rothman
Linda Darling-Hammond

The key word for any kind of educational policy or practice in the United States is *variability*—and this is especially true for teacher education and development. The last 30 years have witnessed a remarkable amount of policy directed at teaching—and an intense debate about whether and how various approaches to preparing and supporting teachers make a difference.

A strong argument for professionalizing teaching was mounted in the mid-1980s with the report of the Carnegie Task Force on Teaching as a Profession (1986), the founding of the reform-minded Holmes Group (1986) of education deans, and the founding of the National Board for Professional Teaching Standards (NBPTS) (n.d.). At that time, researchers, policymakers, and practitioners of teaching and teacher education argued for the centrality of expertise to effective practice and the need to build a more knowledgeable and skillful professional teaching force. A set of policy initiatives was launched to design professional standards, strengthen teacher education and certification, increase investments in induction mentoring and professional development, and transform roles for teachers (e.g., see NCTAF, 1996).

> The key word for any kind of educational policy or practice in the United States is *variability*.

Meanwhile, a competing agenda was introduced to replace the traditional elements of professions—formal preparation, licensure, certification, and accreditation—with market mechanisms that would allow more open entry to teaching and greater ease of termination through elimination of tenure and greater power in the hands of districts to hire and fire teachers with fewer constraints (e.g., see Thomas B. Fordham

Foundation, 1999). Advocates of this perspective have argued that teaching does not require highly specialized knowledge and skill, and that such skills as there are can be learned largely on the job. Teachers would be motivated to work hard and raise student test scores by incentives like merit pay.

Teachers and teacher effectiveness are now at the heart of the education policy agenda in the United States. As a result of federal incentives, more than 30 states have passed laws regarding teacher evaluation in the last few years, and the U.S. Congress is also considering a measure requiring states to evaluate teachers. States have also revamped tenure laws—reducing due process protections and/or lengthening the amount of time until tenure is achieved—and some have reduced the scope of teacher collective bargaining.

In some ways, this focus on teaching at the state and federal levels could be considered a positive sign. It reflects an increased awareness of the importance of teachers and a consensus that ensuring that every student has access to highly effective teachers is a worthwhile goal. Sponsors of many measures cite research showing that teaching is the most important school-related factor in student achievement (Clotfelter et al., 2007; NCTAF, 1996), as well as other research that suggests that highly effective teachers produce significant outcomes for children (Chetty, Friedman, & Rockoff, 2011).

Yet many teachers feel that there is a bull's eye on their backs. Many teachers consider the measures that states and the federal government are considering as punitive—especially those that reduce job protections while attaching teacher evaluation to student test scores. They see them as attempts to hold teachers solely responsible for student performance and to blame them—and get rid of them—when performance falters.

> **Many teachers feel that there is a bull's eye on their backs.**

Partly as a result of these kinds of initiatives, along with declines in pay, increases in class size, and teacher layoffs associated with recent widespread budget cuts, attrition in the teacher workforce has risen sharply at both the beginning and the end of the career. The annual overall attrition rate among teachers rose by 41% from 1988 to 2008, from 6.4% to 9%. The proportion of 1st-year teachers who leave rose from 10% to 13% during that period (Ingersoll & Merrill, 2012).

At least 30% of teachers leave teaching within 5 years (rates are higher in low-income communities), and the profession is relying more and more on less-experienced teachers. Twenty-five years ago the typical teacher was in her 15th year; today the modal teacher is in her 1st or 2nd year, and the median experience level is only 11 years (Carroll & Foster, 2010). A 2011 survey by the MetLife Foundation documented the grim state of the teaching profession: Teachers' job satisfaction was at its lowest point in 2 decades, and more and more teachers expressed a desire to leave teaching (Metlife, 2012).

Educators in Ontario can empathize with their U.S. counterparts. In that province, the government in the 1990s imposed a number of policies teachers considered punitive, such as compulsory tests for new teachers, intensive evaluations, and mandatory professional development. At the same time, as in the United States, budget cuts led to cutbacks in programs and services. Teachers reacted with labor disruptions, including strikes and "work to rule" campaigns, in which they stopped doing extra work beyond their contract hours and obligations. Morale dropped and attrition rose.

The new Ontario provincial government that took office in 2003 reversed many of those policies and established a more cooperative relationship with teachers (see Chapter 4). As a result, there have been no strikes since then, and teaching is once again in demand as a profession. Probably not coincidentally, student performance improved dramatically; now Ontario is one of the best-performing education systems in the world (Levin, 2008; Mehta & Schwartz, 2011).

Could such a transformation happen in the United States? There are some signs of positive developments to grow and support the teaching profession. For example, educator-preparation programs in more than 30 states have piloted a teacher performance assessment that will help ensure that new teachers are qualified to teach effectively (Darling-Hammond, 2013; edTPA, n.d.). A similar assessment in California has produced improvements in teacher education in that state (Darling-Hammond, Newton, & Wei, 2013; Pecheone & Chung, 2006). Similarly, several states have developed ambitious plans for professional development to ensure that teachers are capable of teaching to the Common Core State Standards, which 43 states and the District of Columbia have adopted. The standards call for substantial changes in practice, and states are making significant efforts to help teachers understand the changes and what they mean for instruction.

> Could transformation happen in the United States?

However, these efforts, laudable as they might be, do not add up to a system for ensuring that all students are taught by highly capable and effective teachers. As described in this volume, other countries have put in place such systems, and they have achieved high and equitable levels of student performance.

In this chapter we describe the current landscape of teacher policies in the United States, to show the range of policies in place and under consideration and to analyze their current and potential future effects. Before turning to the policy discussion, we offer a brief overview of the U.S. teaching profession in the early 21st century.

TEACHERS IN THE UNITED STATES

There are about 3.2 million public school teachers in the United States, which makes teaching the second-largest occupation, after retail sales. About three-fourths of teachers are female, 44% are under age 40, and more than half have a master's degree or higher. The median salary for teachers in 2009–2010 was $55,350, which was higher than the median salary for all workers, but less than that of other professions requiring a college degree, such as nurses, accountants, and architects (Ingersoll & Merrill, 2012). According to the Organisation for Economic Co-operation and Development (OECD), U.S. teachers earn only 60% of what the average college graduate earns; in many high-achieving countries, teachers' wages are more equivalent to those earned by other college-educated workers (Schleicher, 2012). These data mask huge variation, however. Teachers in the better-funded New England states tend to be well educated and well paid, while those in the South and Southwest tend to earn much less.

> There are about 3.2 million public school teachers in the United States, which makes teaching the second-largest occupation.

Richard Ingersoll and Lisa Merrill (2012) of the University of Pennsylvania have noted that between 1988 and 2012 the public school teaching force has:

- *"Ballooned:"* The number of teachers has grown faster than the rate of growth in the student population (from 2.3 million to 3.2 million teachers), as the pupil/teacher ratio has shrunk from 17.3 to 15.5. Some of this reduction reflects smaller class sizes in elementary schools and growth in the number of elementary enrichment teachers. In addition, the number of special education teachers doubled between 1988 and 2008. However, with the advent of the Great Recession in 2008, the number of teachers has shrunk by 1%.

- *"Greyed:"* In 1988, the modal age for a teacher was 41; in 2008 it was 55. The number of teachers over age 50 more than doubled in that period, to 1.3 million. Teachers have been retiring, but retirements have likely peaked. Meanwhile, many young teachers have entered the profession, and fewer are staying into mid-career. As a result, the modal age of teachers in 2011–2012 was 30. The teaching force is becoming bimodal—large numbers of young teachers and large numbers of older teachers.

- *"Greened:"* In 2008 there were 239,000 teachers in their 1st year of teaching, as compared with 84,000 in 1988. Not all of the new teachers are fresh out of college; many are mid-career professionals who have switched to teaching. The economic downturn beginning in 2008 slowed this trend, however, as few jobs were available and layoffs often affected younger teachers. In some of the highest-turnover districts, though, there are concerns about having a sufficiently senior teaching force to offer mentoring to younger teachers as well as to maintain the stability and continuity that are needed to sustain school improvement.

> The teaching force is becoming bimodal—large numbers of young teachers and large numbers of older teachers.

- *"Feminized Further:"* Women have long dominated teaching, particularly in the elementary grades, but the proportion of teachers who are female rose from 66% in 1980 to 76% in 2008. Most of the increase occurred in secondary schools.

- *"Diversified:"* The number of teachers of color has doubled since 1987, from 325,000 to 666,000 in 2011, and the proportion of teachers who are members of minority groups rose from 12.4% to 17.3% during that period. However, the proportion of teachers of color remains well below that of the student population; in 2011–2012, 44% of students were members of minority groups. In addition, teachers who are members of minority groups are more likely to leave the profession than White teachers, likely because they tend to teach in high-minority, low-income communities, which have lower salaries, poorer working conditions, and generally higher attrition (see also Adamson & Darling-Hammond, 2012).

While these changes have altered the demographic portrait of the teaching profession, there has also been a consistent and vocal concern about the quality and effectiveness of teachers. In response, policymakers have proposed a range of reforms in recruitment and preparation, career development and pay, and professional development. The following sections describe the current state of American education in those areas and some of the reform efforts under way.

RECRUITMENT AND DISTRIBUTION

Americans have what might be called a schizophrenic view about the selectivity of the teaching profession. On the one hand, many policymakers have expressed the view that teaching should be more selective and have advocated restricting entry into teacher preparation to the most capable prospective teachers. A report by the consulting firm McKinsey and Company bolstered this view. That report stated that high-performing nations such as Finland, Singapore, and South Korea select teacher candidates from among the top third of high school students. In the United States, by contrast, only 23% of all teachers are from the top third of high school students, and only 14% of those in high-poverty schools are drawn from that highly capable group, according to the report (Auguste, Kihn, & Miller, 2010).

The actual qualifications of both other countries' teaching forces and the teacher workforce in the United States are more complex than that report suggested, however. In fact, officials of the National Institute of Education in Singapore have stated that, while teachers in the shrinking undergraduate teacher education program there come from the top third of *high school* students, there are no data about what part of the college distribution sends candidates to the graduate-level preparation programs. By that standard, the United States does equally well, since college-goers are typically among the top half of high school students—and most teachers come from the top half of that distribution (see below), which is the top quarter of the high school population.

A study by Drew H. Gitomer, then of the Educational Testing Service, found that many of the concerns about the academic qualifications of teachers were based on the test scores of high school students who said they intended to become teachers. But many of those students do not end up pursuing teaching.

> In the United States, most teachers come from the top quarter of the high school population.

Looking at the academic background of individuals who actually took teacher licensure tests—and who thus were on their way toward becoming teachers—Gitomer found that prospective teachers, particularly those who were planning to teach academic subject areas (as opposed to elementary education) "had academic abilities that were equal to or higher than those of the general college graduate population" (Gitomer, 2008).

In addition, he found that the academic background of prospective teachers improved substantially between the mid-1990s and the mid-2000s (Gitomer, 2008), as a function of many reforms that set minimum admissions requirements based on grades and competency tests. In most states now, teachers must pass several tests to become licensed, including tests of basic skills, subject matter knowledge, and pedagogy. Those who complete all of these requirements, in addition to a college major, a preparation program, and student teaching, are only a fraction of the individuals who thought they might want to teach at the end of high school. Thus teaching is more selective than most critics suspect.

However, the relative quality of teachers is very much dependent on geography and demographics of students served. States have different standards for entering teaching, and many allow untrained entrants in cases where there are shortages. Because school funding is dramatically unequal within and across states—with the wealthiest districts in the best-funded states spending 10 times per pupil what the poorest ones spend—salaries and working conditions also vary substantially. These, in turn, drive the qualifications of staff that can be hired (Adamson & Darling-Hammond, 2012). School spending, which is tied largely to local tax bases, also generally reflects the populations of children served.

As a result, by every measure of qualification—certification, subject matter background, pedagogical training, selectivity of college attended, test scores, or experience—less-qualified teachers tend to be found in schools serving greater numbers of low-income and minority students (Darling-Hammond, 2010; Lankford, Loeb, & Wyckoff, 2002; Socias, Chambers, Esra, & Shambaugh, 2007). While this is a common pattern, it is not a given. Some states have raised quality, eliminated shortages, and distributed teachers equally, at least for a time, by raising teaching standards and salaries across all districts. Connecticut and North Carolina pursued this course and transformed their teaching forces in the 1990s, substantially increasing student achievement and reducing

> By every measure of qualification, less-qualified teachers tend to be found in schools serving greater numbers of low-income and minority students.

the gaps between more- and less-advantaged students at the same time (Darling-Hammond, 2010).

As part of these reforms, North Carolina's Teaching Fellows Program was perhaps the most highly successful model in the nation for recruiting and preparing highly talented teachers on a large scale. It operated for more than 25 years, bringing more than 10,000 top-achieving recruits into teaching—including a disproportionate number of male and minority candidates—by providing them with full college scholarship loans to teach in the state's public schools for at least 4 years. Studies have found that the recruits stayed in teaching at very high rates: More than 80% remained in teaching after 5 years and many of the remainder moved into public school administration. Furthermore, these teachers were found to be among the most consistently effective in promoting student learning gains (Henry, Bastian, & Smith, 2012).

Unfortunately, political forces intervened, as they typically do in the United States, and this program was repealed in 2012, along with many of North Carolina's other supports for teaching and school leadership. Similarly, some of Connecticut's hard-won gains were later lost due to tax and spending cuts that reduced key programs and allowed funding and teaching gaps to grow again in the poorer districts.

PREPARATION

While many commentators and policymakers have urged teaching to become more selective, others have meanwhile sought to loosen restrictions on teaching to make it easier for people to enter the profession without "barriers" like admissions standards or training. Critics have contended that certification rules erect needless obstacles to prospective teachers by requiring them to complete a specified number of teacher education courses. Not incidentally, reducing entry standards eases shortages in remote districts and districts with lower salaries and more challenging working conditions.

In response to a stream of federal incentives over the last 30 years, nearly every state has established alternative routes to certification that streamline the process and enable would-be teachers to enter the classroom after shortened periods of preservice preparation. Some alternative routes ultimately require all of the same components as traditional preparation, while others drop student teaching and entire areas of study altogether. Overall, about 18% of new high school teachers have entered the profession through alternative routes (U.S. Department of Education, National Center for Education Statistics [NCES], 2007). In all states, these teachers disproportionately teach in low-income or high-minority schools (Darling-Hammond, 2010).

While there are many kinds of alternative routes, those that bypass student teaching and offer little preservice training also appear to have the least productive outcomes for their recruits and the students they teach. Large-scale studies in North Carolina, New York, and Texas found significant negative effects on student achievement for teachers who entered teaching through alternative routes, as compared to fully certified teachers with comparable experience (Boyd, Grossman, Lankford, Loeb, & Wyckoff, 2006; Clotfelter et al., 2007; Darling-Hammond, Holtzman, Gatlin, & Heilig, 2005).

One of the best known alternative routes, Teach for America (TFA), is also aimed at selectivity. TFA recruits prospective teachers from highly selective colleges and universities, and selects "corps members" through a rigorous process of interviews. TFA members participate in a summer training course and are assigned to schools, usually in urban and rural areas, while they complete teacher education programs in nearby universities. Teachers commit to their assignments for 2 years. Research on the effectiveness of TFA teachers has been mixed: Some studies (including those noted above) have found that the recruits are initially less effective than certified beginners, especially at the elementary level and in the teaching of reading (Boyd et al., 2006; Darling-Hammond et al., 2005; Kane, Rockoff, & Staiger, 2006), while others found that they performed comparably with other beginning teachers in their schools (who were also disproportionately likely to be uncertified), and sometimes better in mathematics, especially after their 1st year or 2 in the classroom (Decker, Mayer, & Glazerman, 2004; Xu, Hannaway, & Taylor, 2009).

> Studies in North Carolina, New York, and Texas found significant negative effects on student achievement for teachers who entered teaching through alternative routes.

Studies have tended to find that by the 3rd year, when alternate route teachers have completed their required teacher education coursework for certification, there are few significant differences between their effectiveness and that of the traditionally prepared teachers. However, because these routes typically have high attrition, it is unclear whether the greater effectiveness of later-year recruits is due to selection effects (since studies find that less effective teachers leave earlier) or because the ones who remained have improved their teaching performance with training and experience. (The TFA studies cited earlier, for example, found that more than 80% of TFA entrants and half of other alternatively prepared teachers had left the profession by the end of the 3rd year.)

In addition to the wide range of alternative paths into teaching, there are many types of preservice program options among the 1,400 teacher education programs in the United States: Candidates may prepare in traditional 4-year undergraduate programs; they may spend as much as 5 years preparing to teach in joint programs that provide them with a bachelor's and a master's degree in subject matter and teaching (promoted as part of reforms urged by the Holmes Group of education deans [Holmes Group, 1986, 1990]); or they may pursue a 1- or 2-year master's degree following a separate bachelor's degree, like the Master of Arts in Teaching programs started in elite universities like Harvard, Stanford, and Columbia in the 1960s and 1970s.

These programs differ in structure, content, and quality—and they are regulated differently across the 50 states. In these different programs, candidates generally take courses in subject matter and pedagogy, child development and learning, curriculum and assessment, and the teaching of children with special needs, including students with disabilities and English language learners. However, the course content may vary, and courses may or may not be connected to a clinical experience. The student teaching that candidates experience could be as little as 5 weeks or as many as 30 weeks or more, and might be conducted in a professional development school that is connected to the university and organized for this purpose, or in a random setting that has no claim to enacting state-of-the-art practice or mentoring. As a result of this variability, it is difficult to generalize about teacher education in the United States.

While the structure of programs (undergraduate versus graduate; 4-year versus 5-year) does not appear to be a determinant of quality, other features of programs have been found to make a difference in the later effectiveness of graduates. In particular, studies have found that the most effective programs do several things:

> **It is difficult to generalize about teacher education in the United States.**

- Have a coherent vision that permeates coursework and clinical work
- Emphasize content pedagogy (subject-specific curriculum and teaching methods)

- Connect theory and practice by helping candidates learn specific practices and tools that they apply in classrooms where they are student teaching
- Carefully manage student teaching experiences, selecting mentor teachers and structuring a clinical curriculum so that candidates learn effective practices
- Offer opportunities to study specific curriculum
- Use performance assessments—typically a portfolio of work representing teachers' work in classrooms with students (Boyd, Grossman, Lankford, Loeb, & Wyckoff, 2008; Darling-Hammond, 2006).

Whether programs have these features is partly determined by the rules states set for licensing teachers and for approving preparation programs. (Teachers generally must also pass a test or set of tests and undergo a criminal background check before earning a credential.) In about 15 states these policies are set by a teacher standards board, which usually includes teachers and teacher educators. In the remainder, the state department of education is responsible.

To take a fairly typical example, here are Rhode Island's requirements:

- *Elementary Education:* At least 24 semester hours of education coursework, including coursework in each of the following areas: Child Growth and Development, Methods and Materials of Teaching Math, Science, Social Studies, Reading, Language Arts in the Elementary Schools, The Arts, Identification and Service to Special Needs Children, and Foundations of Education. Six semester hours (12 weeks) of student teaching are required.
- *Secondary Education:* At least 16 semester hours of education coursework, including each of the following areas: Adolescent Psychology, Secondary Methods, Measurements and Evaluation, Identification of and Service to Special Needs Students, Teaching of Reading in the Content Area, and Foundations of Education. For the core academic subjects (mathematics, English, social studies, science, world language), at least 30 semester hours of coursework are required in the subject area to be taught. Six semester hours (12 weeks) of student teaching are required.

In addition to the state requirements, about half of teacher-preparing institutions also pursue accreditation by a national organization, the Council for Accreditation of Teacher Preparation (CAEP). This process also shapes teacher education programs because institutions will revise their programs and offerings to meet CAEP standards. However, the process is voluntary in most states, and many institutions opt not to take part.

CAEP, which was formed in 2010 by the merger of two separate accrediting agencies, the National Council for the Accreditation of Teacher Education (NCATE) and the Teacher Education Accrediting Council (TEAC), is currently putting in place a revised version of its standards. The new accreditation standards place a greater emphasis on longer and better-supervised clinical experience that is more tightly linked to coursework.

> The new accreditation standards place a greater emphasis on longer and better-supervised clinical experience that is more tightly linked to coursework.

One emerging approach emphasizing strong clinical preparation is the residency, which is modeled after medical residency programs. Under that approach, which is operated by school districts such as Boston, Denver, and San Francisco, teachers are recruited carefully and screened. They then work as apprentices for a full year in the classrooms of skilled mentor teachers, while undertaking a fully integrated program of coursework offered by a partnering university. Candidates typically receive this training, which results in a master's degree, for free and receive a living stipend. They also receive mentoring for their first 2 years of practice. In return, they commit to teach for 3 to 5 years in the partnering district's schools. Preliminary evidence suggests that graduates of the residencies outperform traditionally trained teachers over time, and that their retention rates are substantially higher (Berry et al., 2010).

Another initiative under way could have a strong impact on teacher preparation throughout the nation. Following the example of the National Board for Professional Teaching Standards, which developed a performance assessment for certifying accomplished veteran teachers, more than 30 states are currently piloting or fully implementing a performance assessment to be used as a measure for initial licensure. These beginning teacher portfolios require that candidates plan a curriculum unit mapped to their state's learning standards, adapt it for English learners and students with special education needs, teach the unit for several days (capturing a lesson on video), revise their plans based on student learning each day, collect and analyze evidence of student learning, and reflect on next steps needed to extend student learning. Trained scorers who are teachers and teacher educators evaluate this evidence using a set of common rubrics that assess planning, instruction, assessment, and reflection (Darling-Hammond et al., 2013).

The first of these efforts, known as the Performance Assessment for California Teachers (PACT), was found in early studies to predict teachers' later effectiveness in the classroom (Darling-Hammond et al., 2013). The goal of the assessments is to support both candidates' learning and program improvement by offering feedback to programs about what their candidates can do. PACT has already had an effect on preparation programs throughout the state; for example, after PACT results showed that students struggled with classroom assessments and with providing support for English learners, colleges of education revamped their instruction in those areas (Haynes, 2011).

ONGOING PROFESSIONAL DEVELOPMENT

Once teachers enter the profession, most are likely to receive some kind of induction or mentoring support. More than 40 states now offer or require induction programs, though few of them provide funding for mentors. According to the *Teaching and Learning International Survey* (TALIS), an international survey of lower secondary school teachers, about 80% of U.S. principals reported in 2013 that induction programs were available for beginning teachers in their schools, and about 70% of those beginners said they had participated in such programs—above the TALIS average but considerably below the 98% participation rate registered by Singapore (OECD, 2014b). These estimates match U.S. survey data, which further show that, like other opportunities for teachers, induction supports vary considerably by state, with 93% of teachers participating in South Carolina, but only 41% in South Dakota (Wei et al., 2009).

After the induction phase, the nature of ongoing learning opportunities is even more varied. American schools have long offered teachers resources for continued learning and incentives through the salary scale to take advantage of those resources. However, there are continual concerns that the professional development available to teachers is often ineffective.

> Like other opportunities for teachers, induction supports vary considerably by state.

Nearly all schools provide time for professional development for teachers. In a 2000 survey principals said that 95% of public schools offered at least some time for professional development, and 74% of teachers participated; newer teachers were more likely than veterans to take part in professional development (Choy, Chen, & Bugarin, 2006). The time allotted for professional development included time during the school day, days before the school year, common planning time for teachers, and early dismissal time for students. About a third of principals reported reducing teachers' workload in order to provide professional development.

State and local allocations for professional development are highly variable. Wealthier states and districts generally offer more professional learning opportunities; however, districts with significant populations of low-income students receive federal contributions through Title II of the Elementary and Secondary Education Act, which allocates approximately $3 billion a year in grants that can be used to reduce class size or provide professional development.

States and districts also provide incentives for teachers to take part in professional development, by providing additional pay for teachers who earn graduate credits. A study by the Center for American Progress found that, nationwide, the graduate credit amounts to 2.1% of school budgets, or about $174 per pupil (Roza & Miller, 2009). However, the study also noted that there is little correlation between advanced degrees and teacher effectiveness. In part, this is because teachers are traditionally reimbursed for any advanced study, including fields supporting their personal and professional advancement not directly related to teaching, such as counseling or administration. Studies that have found master's degrees to be related to teacher effectiveness have often looked at degrees that are associated with the study of teaching for a credential or with the teaching of a specific subject matter field, such as reading education or mathematics education (Adamson & Darling-Hammond, 2012; Betts, Rueben, & Danenberg, 2000; Goldhaber & Brewer, 1998).

There is evidence that professional development can boost teacher effectiveness. A survey of high-quality research by the Southwest Regional Educational Laboratory found that certain professional development programs boosted student achievement by about 21 percentile points. These were of extended duration (an average of 49 hours on a single area over the course of a year), featuring intensive institutes followed by recurring collegial work and problem solving, and sometimes in-class coaching. However, no study found that professional development training lasting 14 or fewer hours had a positive impact on student achievement (Yoon, Duncan, Lee, Scarloss, & Shapley, 2007).

Unfortunately, much of what U.S. teachers receive falls into this latter category: the one-shot workshop. In most areas in which teachers access professional learning, they spend 8 hours or less on the associated activities (Choy et al., 2006). Even when studying the teaching of their content areas, where professional development access is greatest, fewer than one-quarter of teachers receive sustained professional development of the kind identified in the research as influencing practice (Wei et al., 2009). Not surprisingly, teachers' views of the usefulness of professional development are closely related to the extent to which they have had such an ongoing learning experience (Wei et al., 2009).

> No study found that professional development training lasting 14 or fewer hours had a positive impact on student achievement.

This may explain why relatively few U.S. teachers say that the professional development they have experienced has impacted their practice. A survey of teachers in 2003 found that fewer than half said professional development made them better teachers (Public Agenda, 2003). More recently, the TALIS survey found that, while U.S. teachers tend to participate in professional development at higher rates than their colleagues around the world, only about half felt their teaching methods were influenced by these experiences, fewer than their international peers (OECD, 2014b). TALIS also revealed that U.S. teachers have many more instructional hours and have much less time for job-embedded collaboration and learning than teachers in other countries, which means they have less time for the learning opportunities most valued by teachers.

Some of the most effective professional development does not necessarily receive that label. For example, teachers who have applied for certification by the National Board for Professional Teaching Standards have often said that the process of assembling their teaching portfolio is one of the most powerful professional development

> U.S. teachers have many more instructional hours and have much less time for collaboration and learning than teachers in other countries.

activities they have experienced (Haynes, 1995; NBPTS, 2001). Reflecting on their practice in light of the standards and in consultation with peers has a long-lasting influence on how they think about and engage in teaching.

Similarly, scoring student performance assessments is also a powerful professional activity. By meeting with other teachers and examining student work against standards for performance, teachers gain a better understanding of standards and how to structure classwork to elicit proficient work from students (Darling-Hammond & Falk, 2014). However, despite the potential benefits of scoring assessments, the opportunity remains rare in U.S. classrooms. Most state tests consist largely or exclusively of multiple-choice questions, which are scored by machine; and any open-ended questions are scored in most cases by contractors hired by testing firms.

EVALUATION AND CAREER PATHS

In most states teachers entering the profession earn an initial license, which is provisional. For their first 2 or 3 years on the job, teachers must demonstrate satisfactory performance in order to earn a full, professional license. Once teachers earn full certification, they are generally granted tenure. Although critics contend that tenure is effectively a lifetime job guarantee, that view is erroneous. Tenure ensures that teachers cannot be removed from their jobs without due process. In practice, providing due process can be a lengthy and costly process, and many districts may opt to avoid it. Yet tenured teachers regularly are removed for poor performance, and the high rate of turnover among teachers in their early years suggests that many teachers voluntarily remove themselves.

New Teacher Evaluation Policies

For decades, analysts have found that the evaluation systems used in most states and districts for teachers in the probationary period and afterward are generally weak—contributing little to teacher learning or effective personnel decisionmaking (Toch & Rothman, 2008; Wise et al., 1984). Principals have generally observed teachers once a year for a brief period—teachers often call these "drive-by evaluations"—offer a few comments, and overwhelmingly rate teachers' performance as satisfactory (Toch & Rothman, 2008; Wise et al., 1984).

There are some exceptions to this pattern. One notable exception is TAP: the System for Teacher and Student Advancement (formerly the Teacher Advancement Program), operated by the National Institute for Excellence in Teaching, based in Santa Monica, California. Under that program, which currently is in use with 20,000 teachers across the country, teachers are evaluated five times a year, by both trained observers and their principals, according to clear standards for performance. Based on these evaluations, teachers can receive additional pay or move into positions of greater responsibility, such as coaches and curriculum specialists.

Several dozen other districts, in states as wide-ranging as California, Maryland, Ohio, and Washington, have established peer assistance and review (PAR) systems, in which beginning teachers and veterans who struggle receive intensive support for improvement from mentors in their subject areas. If they fail to improve, they are removed by the decision of a panel comprised of administrators and teachers. These programs have proved successful in supporting timely and effective personnel decisions, and enabling improvement for the relatively small number of teachers who are served by them (Darling-Hammond, 2013).

Concern over the quality of evaluations led the U.S. Education Department to include the issue as a criterion in its 2009 Race to the Top competition. In response to the competition, which offered winning states a share of $4 billion in federal funds, more than half the states passed laws to create or revamp evaluation systems. At federal insistence, these laws required, for the first time, that student achievement count in teachers' evaluations—in many cases, as much as 50% of a teacher's ratings. The use of student test score data in teachers' evaluations has long been extremely controversial. Student achievement is the product of many factors, most of which teachers have little or no control over, such as students' home and family contexts, their health and other personal factors, their other prior and current teachers, and school resources ranging from books, class size, and curriculum, to the availability of reading specialists. Indeed, researchers have found that teachers account for only about 7–10% of the variance in student learning (Goldhaber, Brewer, & Anderson, 1999; Rivkin, Hanushek, & Kain, 2000).

Faced with such concerns, researchers have attempted to account for factors outside teachers' control and isolate the effects of teachers on student learning through the use of *value-added* modeling. Simply put, value-added models seek to take into account students' background and prior achievement and predict how a student would perform based on his or her previous trajectory of learning. If the student performs above what was predicted, the teacher added value. If the student performed below the prediction, the teacher's value-added was negative.

> Teachers account for only about 7–10% of the variance in student learning.

Yet value-added scores are notoriously unreliable and error-prone. Teachers' ratings vary from test to test, class to class, and year to year. One study, for example, found that, among teachers who were in the bottom 20% on value-added ratings one year, only 20% to 30% had similar ratings the following year. Between 25% and 45% of the low-rated teachers were in the top group the next year. These shifts do not occur because teachers become remarkably effective overnight. Rather, the ratings are volatile because of the composition of the teachers' classrooms, features of the tests that are used, and other factors that have nothing to do with teachers' skill (Darling-Hammond, Amrein-Beardsley, Haertel, & Rothstein, 2012; McCaffrey et al., 2004; Newton, Darling-Hammond, Haertel, & Thomas, 2010). Studies have found that, because teachers typically receive lower value-added ratings in the years when they are assigned greater numbers of high-need students, value-added models not only misrepresent teachers' actual effectiveness; they also discourage teachers from teaching the students most in need of expert instruction.

Despite these concerns, the federal government has continued to require the use of value-added models in teacher evaluations. And some districts have gone further and released teachers' value-added ratings to the public. In a notorious incident in 2010, the *Los Angeles Times* obtained the value-added scores of teachers in that city, and with the help of a researcher, ranked teachers according to their scores. The newspaper then published the results. Later, other researchers found that different statistical methods would produce dramatically different ratings for individual teachers (Briggs & Domingue, 2011). The same thing happened in New York City in 2012. These events have added to the sense of outrage many teachers feel and may have contributed to the reduced attractiveness of the profession.

> Value-added models discourage teachers from teaching the students most in need of expert instruction.

Career Development and Compensation

Most of the discussion about teacher evaluation is focused on removing low-performers from the profession. In very few cases is there an intention for new evaluation systems to be used for career development or recognition. In countries such as Singapore evaluations are used to help direct teachers into career pathways. Depending on their interests, teachers judged as highly effective can advance in their careers in schools, either by taking on additional roles such as coach or curriculum specialist, or by entering school administration (see Chapter 4). The United States, for the most part, lacks such pathways. Some systems, such as TAP, have created career options for teachers and use evaluations as a way of finding the teachers best suited to advance. But in most districts, with the exception of some opportunities to mentor beginners, the job description of a veteran teacher is the same as that of a neophyte. Effective teachers seldom advance unless they want to leave the classroom and go into administration.

Similarly, there are few places with differentiated pay systems that reward highly effective teachers with higher salaries. Some states and districts recognize the achievement of National Board Certification in their pay scales. Fewer than 10% offer financial incentives for teachers in subject areas where there are shortages (e.g., mathematics, science, and special education) or for teachers who teach in high-need communities. Otherwise, the pay system used almost universally in the United States has been aimed at reducing disparities in pay by creating a single scale that grants raises based on the number of years a teacher works and additional educational credits. That system was created in Des Moines and Denver in the 1920s to eliminate the inequities that had characterized teacher pay up to that point; male teachers tended to earn much more than female teachers, White teachers earned more than Black teachers, and raises depended on the whims of the principal.

Various kinds of adjustments to the single salary schedule have been urged by proponents seeking to address supply and demand variables and those who want to reward performance. The federal government has spurred these efforts through a program known as the Teacher Incentive Fund, which has funded new pay systems in about 100 districts (of 15,000 nationwide) since its inception in 2006. The results of the new systems have been mixed. One of the best-known of these new systems was launched in Denver, one of the original sites of the single salary schedule. Denver's system, known as Professional Compensation, or ProComp, rewards teachers who meet student-growth objectives, who demonstrate improvements in knowledge and skills, and who teach in hard-to-serve assignments or hard-to-staff schools. The system in Denver includes both additional compensation and master teacher roles that involve the transfer of expertise. Initial evidence suggests that ProComp has contributed to improved student achievement in Denver (Wiley, Spindler, & Subert, 2010).

TAP also provides additional pay to teachers who are rated effective through observations and measures of student learning. These teachers, too, are eligible for leadership roles that support teaching within the school. Research conducted by the organization that operates TAP suggested that the program has resulted in improvements in student learning, at least in elementary school. An independent study of TAP in Chicago, however, found no effects on student achievement, although the study did find that teachers in TAP schools were more likely than those in comparison schools to remain in teaching (Glazerman & Seifullah, 2012).

Elsewhere, experiments in pay for performance have shown little effect on student achievement. A closely watched, rigorously conducted study in Nashville found that providing bonuses to teachers for improvements in student test scores did not produce higher levels of student learning (Springer et al., 2010). A similar study of a performance-pay program in New York City, which offered bonuses to entire school faculties rather than to individual teachers, similarly found no improvement in student achievement, and the program was scrapped (Marsh et al., 2011).

> Experiments in pay for performance for teachers have shown little effect on student achievement.

However, the studies did not examine whether the programs resulted in a change in the composition of the teaching workforce. Some advocates of pay-for-performance systems have argued that such schemes would encourage more-able people to enter the teaching profession with the promise of reward for higher performance. However, many teachers have stated that they are insulted by the idea that they would only work hard for students in order to earn more money, and teachers in Florida burned their merit pay checks before the system there was repealed. So it is not clear that these kinds of schemes serve as a motivator for teachers.

SCHOOL LEADERSHIP

As this chapter suggests, policymakers have typically responded to demands for school reform by focusing their attention almost exclusively on areas that have an obvious direct connection to student learning: teacher recruitment, training, credentialing, and evaluation, as well as curriculum, testing, and accountability. Many of these legislative efforts have increased the demands on principals by requiring implementation or monitoring at the school site, without increasing principals' knowledge and capacities to manage the reforms. The significant role of the principal in creating the conditions for improved student outcomes began to be recognized in the 1990s; however, the ability of principals to rise to the ever-increasing demands of each additional reform effort was often taken for granted.

As the importance of leadership to school success has become increasingly evident, policymakers have placed greater demands on principals. Between 1975 and 1990, the number of states with state-mandated principal evaluations increased from 9 to 40 (Snyder & Ebmeier, 1992). In 1996 a consortium of states called the Interstate Leadership Licensing Consortium (ISLLC) translated the new leadership expectations into standards for principal preparation and licensing to guide preservice programs and, in some states, new assessments for principal licensing. More than 40 states have adopted or adapted these standards, and some have developed performance assessments to evaluate candidates' acquisition of the skills they outline. State, national, and international investments in inservice training of principals increased during the period (Hallinger, 1992; Murphy, 1990). New leadership development programs have been launched by some foundations as well as states and districts. Principals are more likely to have formal training for their positions in the United States than in many other countries (OECD, 2014b).

Even so, these initiatives provide a spotty landscape of supports across the country. A few states and districts have moved aggressively to overhaul their systems of preparation and inservice development for principals, making systemic investments that have been sustained. Others have introduced individual programmatic initiatives without system changes. Similarly, some universities or other program providers have dramatically transformed the programs they offer, while others have made marginal changes.

A consensus about the features of successful programs has begun to develop. As outlined in a recent review of the research (Davis, Darling-Hammond, LaPointe, & Meyerson, 2005), strong leadership development programs tend to feature many of the same qualities that characterize strong teacher education programs:

> A consensus about the features of successful preparation programs for school leaders has begun to develop.

- *Research-based content* that includes learning and instruction, the development of quality teaching and professional learning, organizational development, data analysis, and change management, as well as leadership skills
- *Curricular coherence* that links goals, learning activities, and candidate assessments around a set of standards for leadership competence
- *Problem-based learning methods* that connect theory and practice and teach effective problem-framing and problem-solving strategies

- *Field-based internships or coaching* that connects intellectual work with practical work under the guidance of an expert practitioner who can model good practice, coach another practitioner, ask probing questions to guide reflection, and provide feedback to guide the development of practice
- *Cohort groups* that create opportunities for collaboration and teamwork in practice-oriented situations
- *Close collaboration* between programs and school districts, so that the work of the program is directly linked to the instructional efforts of the schools

State initiatives have often sought to incorporate some of these features in accreditation requirements for preservice programs and the design of inservice programs. A number of districts have created innovative partnerships with local universities to strengthen preservice and inservice preparation of principals, and some states have undertaken new initiatives to support stronger preparation for principals and other school leaders, emphasizing in particular their roles as instructional leaders and organizational change agents. In some of these cases, rather than waiting to see who signs up for principal credentialing programs, districts and universities have sought out and identified dynamic teachers who have demonstrated leadership qualities for development as school principals. In the best cases—for instance, in Delaware, Mississippi, and North Carolina—states then provide funding to ensure that these individuals receive high-quality preparation and mentoring.

WHAT'S MISSING? A SYSTEM

States and the federal government have pursued a wide range of initiatives to improve the quality and effectiveness of teaching in the United States. As noted above, these initiatives for the most part reflect a consensus that strengthening the educator workforce and ensuring that all students have access to teachers who are capable and caring is the most powerful way to improve student learning. An education system can only be as strong as its teachers.

> An education system can only be as strong as its teachers.

However, as with most areas of education policy in the United States, these efforts have taken place in most cases in a somewhat haphazard, stop-and-start fashion. Policymakers have tended to focus on one area—say, teacher evaluation—without, apparently, much consideration for how those changes would affect another area—say, retention. And there have been few efforts to focus on a *system* for improving the teacher workforce. As Marc S. Tucker (2011) put it,

> In fact, examples of excellent practice in almost every area of importance can be found in the United States. But my aim here is not to focus on isolated examples of good practice, but, rather, on the *policy systems* that make for effective *education systems* at scale. For this is where the United States comes up short. (p. 170)

There are some noteworthy exceptions to this rule. In the mid-1980s, both Connecticut and North Carolina enacted the most substantial and systemic investments in teaching of any state. These states, both of which serve large high-poverty student populations, coupled major statewide increases in teacher salaries and improvements in teacher salary equity with increases in teacher standards. They launched intensive recruitment efforts and initiatives to improve preservice teacher and principal education, licensing, beginning teacher mentoring, and ongoing professional development, including the use of teacher performance assessments.

Many of the successful initiatives we have described in this chapter grew out of these major reforms. North Carolina's Teaching Fellows program was the first to recruit hundreds of able high school students into teacher preparation each year by entirely subsidizing their college education; the state later launched a comparable Principals Fellows program for training administrators. The state created professional development academies for teachers and principals and underwrote teacher development networks like the National Writing Project and an analogous set of professional development initiatives in mathematics, launched a beginning teacher mentoring program that included a portfolio for guiding teacher learning, and introduced the most wide-ranging set of incentives in the nation for teachers to pursue National Board Certification, including incorporation of this accomplishment into the salary schedule.

Connecticut was the first state to build performance-based assessments for beginning teachers and principals, following on the portfolio developed by the National Board, and to create a state-funded mentoring program that supported trained mentors for beginning teachers. These were integrated into reforms of teacher education that increased teachers' learning of subject matter, content pedagogy, reading, and special education, and encouraged universities to establish professional development schools to support clinical training. They were accompanied by investments in an intensive professional development program in mathematics, science, and technology that offered 4-week institutes with follow-up support to teachers.

By the late 1990s, once-low-performing North Carolina had posted the largest student achievement gains in mathematics and reading of any state in the nation. Higher-achieving Connecticut also posted significant gains, becoming one of the top-scoring states in the nation on the National Assessment of Educational Progress in every subject matter, despite an increase in the proportion of low-income and limited English proficient students during that time (Darling-Hammond, 2010).

However, a tax revolt in Connecticut and changes in governance at the state level in both states have caused these systemic approaches to unravel over the last decade, and many of these successful initiatives have been untended or even repealed. This, too, is one of the challenges of the highly politicized education environment in the United States. Even when successful policy is made, it is difficult to protect it for very long.

What would it take to develop and maintain policies that produce an effective education system? One promising first step would be to examine the policies and practices of education systems that appear to be most effective at improving outcomes for young people, and doing so in an equitable fashion—and that have sustained progress for a significant period of time. The following chapters provide a detailed look at three such systems.

CHAPTER 3

Developing Effective Teachers and School Leaders

The Case of Finland

Pasi Sahlberg

With its high levels of educational achievement and attainment, Finland is regarded as one of the world's most literate societies. All children in Finland have the right to high-quality early childhood education in public, private, or home-based kindergarten or day care. Some 75% of 3- to 5-year-olds are in full-day early childhood programs. More than 98% of Finns attend preschool at the age of 6; 99% complete compulsory basic education at the age of 16, and 95% of these go on to academic or vocational upper secondary schools. About 95% of those who start the academic strand of upper secondary school at age 16 graduate. Completion rates in vocational upper secondary school also reach close to 90%. Finland's publicly funded higher education system offers tuition-free study to over 60% of the age cohort annually (Statistics Finland, n.d.).

Since it emerged in 2000 as the top-scoring Organisation for Economic Co-operation and Development (OECD) nation on the Program for International Student Assessment (PISA) tests, researchers have been pouring into the country to study the so-called Finnish miracle. How did a country with an undistinguished education system in the 1980s surge to the head of the global class in just a few decades? Research and experience suggest that one element of the Finnish system trumps all others: excellent teachers and leaders. This chapter looks at how Finland develops such excellence in its educator workforce.

THE TEACHER IN FINNISH SOCIETY

Education has always been an integral part of Finnish culture and society. Teachers currently enjoy great respect and trust in Finland. Finns regard teaching as a noble, prestigious profession—akin to medicine, law, or economics—and one, like medicine, driven by moral purpose rather than material interests.

It is no wonder, then, that teaching is one of the most popular career choices among young Finns. The Finnish media regularly report results of opinion polls that document favorite professions among general upper secondary school graduates. Teaching is consistently rated as one of the most admired professions, ahead of medical doctors, architects, and lawyers, typically thought to be dream professions (Liiten, 2004). Teaching is congruent with the core social values of Finns, which include social justice, caring for others, and happiness, as reported by the regular National Youth Surveys in Finland. Teaching is also regarded as an independent profession that enjoys public respect and praise. It is particularly popular among young women—90% of those accepted for study in primary teacher education programs are female (Finnish National Board of Education, n.d.).

> Finns regard teaching as a noble, prestigious profession—akin to medicine, law, or economics.

There is another interesting perspective on the status of the teaching profession in Finland. In a national opinion survey, about 1,300 adult Finns (ages 15 to 74) were asked if their spouse's (or partner's) profession had influenced their decision to commit to a relationship with them (Kangasniemi, 2008). Interviewees were asked to select 5 professions from a list of 30 that they would prefer for a selected partner or spouse. The responses were rather surprising. Finnish males viewed a teacher as the most desirable spouse, rated just ahead of a nurse, medical doctor, or architect. Women, in turn, identified only a medical doctor and a veterinarian ahead of a teacher as a desirable profession for their ideal husband. In the entire sample, 35% rated teacher as among the top five preferred professions for their ideal spouse. Apparently, only medical doctors are more sought after in Finnish mating markets than teachers. This clearly documents both the high professional and social status that teachers have attained in Finland—both in and out of schools.

Teachers also are the main reason Finland now leads the international pack in literacy, science, and math. Until the 1960s the level of educational attainment in Finland remained fairly low: Only 1 in 10 adult Finns had completed more than 9 years of basic education, and achieving a university degree was uncommon (Sahlberg, 2010). Back then, Finland's education level was comparable with that of Malaysia or Peru, and lagged behind its Scandinavian neighbors of Denmark, Norway, and Sweden. Today, Finland publicly recognizes the value of its teachers and trusts their professional judgment in schools. Without excellent teachers, Finland's current international success would have been impossible to achieve.

The Finnish education system does not employ external standardized student testing to drive the performance of schools. Neither does it employ a rigorous inspection system of schools and teachers. Instead of test-based accountability, the Finnish system relies on the expertise and professional trust–based responsibility of teachers who are knowledgeable and committed to their students and communities.

RECRUITING THE BEST

Becoming a primary school teacher in Finland is a very competitive process. Only Finland's best and most committed are able to fulfill those professional dreams. Every spring, more than 8,000 high school graduates submit their applications to the departments of teacher education in Finnish research universities that prepare primary school teachers. Usually it is not enough to complete high school and pass a rigorous matriculation examination. Successful candidates must also have excellent interpersonal skills and a deep personal commitment to teach and work in schools. Annually only about 1 in every 10 applicants will be accepted to study to become a primary school teacher. Among all categories of teacher education, ranging from kindergarten teachers to adult education teachers, about 5,000 teacher candidates are selected from over 20,000 applicants.

The primary school teacher education program is the most popular, and therefore also the most competitive in terms of intake. Primary school teacher education is based on a master's degree that is offered by eight of Finland's research universities. Academic requirements meet common program standards, but the details of the curriculum are determined at the university level. The content and methods of these primary school teacher education programs vary from university to university, but the overall standards are the same for all providers.

The entry procedure to the primary teacher education programs emphasizes candidates' abilities to succeed in teacher education rather than looking only at prior grades. This examination is based on a set of scientific and professional articles that are announced and made available to students in late March. In 2014 there were six articles to be read

> 5,000 teacher candidates are selected from over 20,000 applicants.

for the exam, and they covered a wide range of issues, such as "Development and assessment of working memory in childhood," "Equality and justice in basic education placement and selectivity," and "Change in education policy and school's position in Europe." Based on students' performance in this exam, a subset of candidates is then invited to the second phase of the selection process, which varies from one university to another.

In the second phase, one that more deeply explores candidates' qualifications at an earlier stage than many systems, candidates are often asked to plan and engage in an observed activity with a small group of other candidates simulating real classroom situations. This helps the admission committee see candidates' creative thinking, interpersonal skills, and other aspects of personality that are considered to be important in the teaching profession. Finally, potential candidates go through an individual interview where more details of their dispositions, prior experiences working with children, and commitments to teaching are closely examined.

These highly capable candidates then complete a rigorous teacher education program at government expense.

The salary level is not the main motive to become a teacher in Finland. Teachers earn slightly more than the Finnish national average salary. The annual teacher's salary, by statute, in the upper grades of comprehensive school (grades 7 through 9) after 15 years of experience (in equivalent U.S. dollars converted by using purchasing-power parity) is about 42,600 USD (OECD, 2014a). That is close to what teachers earn, on average, in OECD countries. The comparable annual salary in the United States is 47,000 USD, and in Korea, 50,000 USD. However, the Finnish teacher's salary is more comparable to that of other college-educated workers in that country than is true of the U.S. teacher's salary.

> Highly capable candidates complete a rigorous teacher education program at government expense.

Although making money is not the main reason for becoming a teacher, there are systematic ways for salaries to increase. Finnish teachers climb the salary ladder as their teaching experience grows, reaching the peak after about 20 years of service. The same salary scheme is applied nationwide and is determined in a national labor contract that the Trade Union of Education negotiates with the Local Government Employers Confederation.

However, there are a number of factors that affect the paycheck. First, teacher pay depends on the type of school (e.g., primary or upper secondary school). Although teachers' pay in Finland is not linked to their students' achievement in any way, the salary structure is based on merit and performance. Basic salary includes the base pay determined in the labor contract and an addition determined locally depending on particular skills, responsibilities, social skills, and working conditions that may vary greatly from school to school. Next, there is a personal bonus in each teacher's salary that depends on overall job performance. Then there is extra pay from additional hours included on top of the minimum required teaching load, together with other possible compensation. This includes 3 weekly hours for collaboration, school improvement, or other collegial activities. Finally, teachers may receive a performance bonus awarded to their school or cluster of schools as a collective reward for especially successful work accomplished together. As a consequence, there may be variation in teachers' earnings even within the same school, depending on seniority, the nature of their work, and overall performance that is normally judged by the principal.

PREPARING THEM WELL

All teachers in Finnish primary, lower secondary, and upper secondary schools must hold a master's degree; preschool and kindergarten teachers must hold a bachelor's degree. There are no alternative ways to receive a teacher's diploma in Finland; the university degree constitutes a license to teach.

Primary school teachers major in education, while upper-grade teachers concentrate their studies in a particular subject, such as mathematics, as well as didactics, consisting of pedagogical content knowledge specific to that subject.

Teacher education is based on a combination of research, practice, and reflection, meaning that it must be supported by scientific knowledge and focus on thinking processes and cognitive skills used in conducting research. In addition to studying educational theory, content, and subject-specific pedagogy, each student completes a master's thesis on a topic relevant to educational practice. Successful completion of a master's degree in teaching (including a bachelor's degree) generally takes 5 to 7.5 years, depending on the field of study (Ministry of Education, 2007).

> There are no alternative ways to receive a teacher's diploma in Finland.

Strong Focus on Content and Pedagogy

A broad-based curriculum ensures that newly prepared Finnish teachers possess balanced knowledge and skills in both theory and practice. It also means that prospective teachers possess deep professional insight into education from several perspectives, including educational psychology and sociology, curriculum theories, student assessment, special-needs education, and pedagogical content knowledge in selected subject areas. All eight universities that offer teacher education in Finland have their own strategies and curricula that are nationally coordinated to ensure coherence but locally crafted in order to make the best use of the particular university's resources.

Subject teachers complete a master's degree in one major subject and one or two minor subjects. Students then apply to a university's department of teacher education to study pedagogy for their focus subject. Subject-focused pedagogy and research are advanced in Finnish universities, and strategies of cooperative and problem-based learning, reflective practice, and computer-supported education are common.

A higher education evaluation system that rewards effective, innovative university teaching practice has served as an important driver for these developments. Finland's Center for Evaluation of Education carries out independent reviews of Finnish universities and their programs, research, and teaching. High-performing units (i.e., faculties, departments, or programs) receive rewards that include national recognition and an additional monetary bonus from the Ministry of Education and Culture. Finland's teacher education was reviewed last in 2000 by an international panel as part of the higher education evaluation policy in Finland (Jussila & Saari, 2000).

Integration of Theory, Research, and Practice

Finland's commitment to research-based teacher education means that educational theories, research methodologies, and practice all play an important role in preparation programs (Jakku-Sihvonen & Niemi, 2006; Westbury, Hansen, Kansanen, & Björkvist, 2005). Teacher education curricula are designed to create a systematic pathway from the foundations of educational thinking to educational research methodologies and then on to the more advanced field of the educational sciences. Each student thereby builds an understanding of the systemic nature of educational practice. Finnish students also learn the skills of how to design, conduct, and present original research on practical or theoretical aspects of education.

Another important element of Finnish research-based teacher education is practical training in schools, which is a key component of the curriculum, integrated with research and theory. Over the 5-year program, candidates advance from basic teaching practice to advanced practice and then to final practice. During each of these phases, students observe lessons by experienced teachers, practice teaching observed by supervisory teachers, and deliver independent lessons to different groups of pupils while being evaluated by supervising teachers and department of teacher education professors and lecturers. Practicum experiences comprise about 15 to 20% of teachers' overall preparation time. Within the 5 to 7 years of the combined bachelor's- and master's-level preparation, at least a full year of practicum experiences occurs.

Much of this practicum work is completed within special Teacher Training Schools governed by the universities. These schools have similar curricula and practices to normal public schools. However, teachers in these schools become part of the university faculty, along with the university's professors, lecturers, and researchers who work in departments of teacher education. Some student teachers also practice teach in a network of selected Municipal Field Schools, which are regular public schools. Schools where practice teaching occurs have higher professional staff requirements, and supervising teachers have to prove they are competent to work with student teachers.

Teacher Training Schools are also expected to pursue research and development roles in collaboration with the university department of teacher education and sometimes with the academic faculties who also have teacher education functions. These schools can, therefore, introduce sample lessons and alternative curricular designs to student teachers. These schools also have teachers who are well prepared in supervision and teacher professional development and assessment strategies. Because initial teacher education has a strong focus on linking theory into practice, Finnish teachers are well prepared for taking a teaching job as soon as they are assigned to a school.

> Practicum experiences comprise about 15 to 20% of teachers' overall preparation time, [totaling] at least a full year.

> Finnish teachers are well prepared for taking a teaching job as soon as they are assigned to a school.

HIRING, EVALUATION, AND RETENTION

Because Finland has no centralized management of education, the school and the principal, together with the school board, typically make hiring decisions. Small allowances or premiums are offered to attract young teachers to teach in small rural schools, which are generally less popular than those in the urban areas near the universities where teachers have studied. The teaching force in Finland is highly unionized; almost all teachers are members of the Trade Union of Education.

There is no formal teacher evaluation in Finland. Teachers receive feedback from their principal and the school staff itself. Because Finland does not have a standardized assessment for evaluating students, there is no formal consideration of student learning outcomes in the evaluation. Teacher and leader effectiveness are defined using a broader meaning of student learning than just test scores in mathematics and reading literacy.

> Teacher and leader effectiveness are defined using a broader meaning of student learning than test scores.

Once a teacher has permanent employment in a school, there are no checkpoints or means for terminating a contract unless there is a violation of the ethical rules of teaching. Finland relies on the strong preparation of teachers, their professional ethic, and their opportunities for ongoing engagement with colleagues in the professional work of teaching and curriculum and assessment development to support their effectiveness. A good teacher is one who is able to help all children progress and grow in a holistic way.

When new teachers are employed in a school, they usually stay there for life. Very few primary school teachers leave their work during the first 5 years, and attrition is much less common than in other countries. An official estimate suggests that only 10% to 15% of teachers leave the profession during the course of their career.

Teachers compare what they do in a primary school classroom to the work that doctors do in medical clinics. A key characteristic of Finnish teachers' work environment is that they are autonomous, trusted, and respected professionals. Unlike nations that have bureaucratic accountability systems that make teachers feel threatened, overcontrolled, and undervalued, teaching in Finland is a very sophisticated profession, where teachers feel they can truly exercise the skills they have learned in the

> Test-based accountability is replaced by trust-based responsibility and inspiration for human development.

university. Test-based accountability is replaced by trust-based responsibility and inspiration for human development.

PROFESSIONAL LEARNING AND DEVELOPMENT

Finnish teachers possessing a master's degree have the right to participate in postgraduate studies to supplement their professional development. Many teachers take advantage of the opportunity to pursue doctoral studies in education, often while simultaneously teaching school. For doctoral studies in education, students must complete advanced learning in the educational sciences.

While Finnish teacher education has been praised for its systematic academic structure and high overall quality (Jussila & Saari, 2000), professional development and inservice programs for teachers are more variable. In Finland, induction of new teachers into their first teaching position is less uniform than initial preparation. It is up to each school and municipality to take care of new teachers' induction to their teaching assignments. Some schools, as part of their mission, have adopted advanced procedures and support systems for new staff, whereas other schools simply bid new teachers welcome and show them their classrooms. In some schools, induction is a specific responsibility of school principals or deputy principals, while in others, induction jobs may be assigned to experienced teachers.

An issue that is well known in Finland is that teachers' professional development and school improvement programs are not well aligned with initial teacher education and often lack focus on essential areas of teaching and educational development. Municipalities, as the overseers of primary and lower and upper secondary schools, are responsible for providing teachers with opportunities for professional development, based on their needs. Perhaps the main criticism deals with weak coordination between initial academic teacher education and the continuing professional development of teachers (Ministry of Education, 2009).

According to the teachers' employment contract, there are 3 mandatory professional development days annually that are offered by the local education authorities. It is up to individual teachers or school principals to decide how much time beyond those 3 days and what type of professional development is needed, and whether such interventions, in fact, can be funded.

In Finland a significant disparity exists among municipalities' and schools' ability to finance professional development for teachers. The main reason for this situation is the way that education is financed. The central government has only a limited influence on budgetary decisions made by municipalities or schools. Therefore, some schools receive significantly more allocations for professional development and school improvement than do others, particularly during times of economic downturn when professional development budgets are often the first to vanish.

Governance of Finnish education differs from one municipality to the next. Some schools experience relatively high autonomy over their operations and budgeting. Others do not. Therefore, Finnish teacher professional development appears in many forms. Ideally, the school is the prime decisionmaker regarding the design and delivery of professional development. Schools may also be motivated to lower operating expenses, such as for textbooks, heating, and maintenance, and may divert those funds to teacher development priorities. However, some Finnish municipalities still organize professional development programs uniformly for all teachers and allow little latitude for individual schools to decide what would be more beneficial for them. According to a national survey conducted by the University of Jyväskylä in 2007, on average, teachers devoted about 7 working days (or 50 hours) annually to professional development; approximately half of that was drawn from teachers' personal time (Piesanen, Kiviniemi, & Valkonen, 2007).

According to the 2013 National Teacher Survey (National Board of Education, 2014) more than 80% of Finnish teachers had participated in some type of professional development during the past year. OECD's TALIS survey in 2013 confirmed that trend: The participation rate in professional development was 79% among Finnish lower secondary teachers. In this, Finland is lagging behind many other countries—the OECD average in that survey was 88% (OECD, 2014b). The Finnish Ministry of Education would like to increase teacher participation in professional development (Ministry of Education, 2009). The government, therefore, is considering ways to strengthen the legal grounds for teacher professional development by requiring that all teachers must have access to adequate professional development support, funded by municipalities.

The Finnish state budget normally allocates about 30–40 million USD each year to the professional development of teachers and school principals through various forms of university courses and professional development. The main purpose of this investment in human capital is to ensure equal access to further training, particularly for teachers who work in more disadvantaged schools. This professional development support is contracted to service providers on a competitive basis. The government initially determines the focus of the desired training, based on current national educational development needs. Local education authorities that own the schools and employ all the teachers make an investment of similar scale in the professional development of their education personnel each year. The Ministry of Education, in collaboration with municipalities, plans to double public funding for teacher professional development by 2016.

ENGAGEMENT IN CURRICULUM AND ASSESSMENT DEVELOPMENT

During the course of Finland's education reforms, teachers have demanded more autonomy and responsibility for curriculum and student assessment (Aho, Pitkänen, & Sahlberg, 2006). Gradual growth of teacher professionalism in Finnish schools since the 1980s has made this a legitimate appeal. Teachers' engagement in these areas contributes to teacher status, satisfaction, and effectiveness.

While the *National Core Curriculum for Basic Education* and similar documents for upper secondary education provide guidance to teachers, curriculum planning is the responsibility of schools and municipalities. Local education authorities and teachers approve the school-level curriculum, and school principals play a key role in curriculum design. Teacher education provides them with well-developed curriculum knowledge and planning skills. Moreover, the importance of curriculum design in teacher practice has helped shift the focus of professional development from fragmented professional development toward more systemic, theoretically grounded, schoolwide improvement efforts.

Along with curriculum design, teachers play a key role in assessing students. Finnish schools do not use standardized testing to determine student success. There are three primary reasons for this. First, while assessment practice is well grounded in the National Curriculum, education policy in Finland gives a high priority to personalized learning and creativity as an important part of how schools operate. Therefore, the progress of each student in school is judged more against his or her individual development and abilities rather than against statistical indicators. Second, education authorities insist that curriculum, teaching, and learning, rather than testing, should drive teachers' practice in schools. Student assessment in Finnish schools is embedded in the teaching and learning process and used to improve both teachers' and students' work throughout the academic year. Third,

> Finnish schools do not use standardized testing to determine student success.

determining students' academic performance and social development in Finland is seen as a responsibility of the school, not the external assessors. Teachers are the best judges of how their own students are progressing in school.

Finnish schools accept that there may be some limitations on comparability when teachers do all the grading. At the same time, Finns believe that the problems often associated with external standardized testing—narrowing of the curriculum, teaching to the test, unethical practices related to manipulating test results, and unhealthy competition among schools—can be more problematic. Since Finnish teachers must design and conduct appropriate curriculum-based assessments to document student progress, classroom assessment and school-based evaluation are important parts of teacher education and professional development.

Although Finnish teachers' work consists primarily of classroom teaching, many of their duties lie outside of class. Formally, teachers' working time in Finland consists of classroom teaching, preparation for class, and 2 hours a week planning schoolwork with colleagues. From an international perspective, Finnish teachers devote less time to teaching than do teachers in many other nations. For example, a typical middle school teacher in Finland teaches just under 600 hours annually. In the United States, by contrast, a teacher at the same level devotes 1,080 hours to teaching or teaching-related activities during 180 school days (OECD, 2014b). This means that a typical middle school teacher in the United States spends much more time teaching or working with students compared with his or her counterpart in Finland. Finnish middle school teachers typically teach about four or five 45-minute lessons daily. Students in Finland have shorter school days and more recess time every day than their peers in the U.S. schools. In elementary schools, pupils have four or five 45-minute lessons a day, and in middle school five or six daily lessons. Finnish students typically have less homework than their peers in many other countries. A commonly heard response from Finnish middle school students regarding their daily homework load is about half an hour.

This, however, does not imply that teachers in Finland work less than teachers in other countries. An important—and still voluntary—part of Finnish teachers' work is devoted to the improvement of classroom practice, the advancement of the school as a whole, and work with the community (Sahlberg, 2015). Because Finnish teachers take on significant responsibility for curriculum and assessment, as well as experimentation with and improvement of teaching methods, some of the most important aspects of their work are conducted outside of classrooms.

CAREER DEVELOPMENT AND LEADERSHIP

Because teaching is highly professionalized, diverse responsibilities are handled within the teaching role. An unusual feature of Finnish schools is that all the teachers are equal and are expected to do similar types of things. It is very rare for anyone to be assigned to a strictly nonteaching role. Job portfolios may differ—teachers may have some type of special role in working with the curriculum or parent–school cooperation or business–school partnership—but everybody still teaches.

If teachers have a special role that is particularly time-consuming, they still continue to teach, perhaps with fewer teaching hours. Rarely do these roles receive additional compensation. Occasionally, principals may offer a small stipend to teachers who are doing other work in addition to their teaching. However, the relative difference between salaries of beginning and senior teachers is much larger in Finland than in the United States (OECD, 2014b).

> The relative difference between salaries of beginning and senior teachers is much larger in Finland than in the United States.

DEVELOPMENT OF SCHOOL LEADERS

By law, all school principals must be qualified teachers for the school they lead and must complete a specific course of academic training at the university. In most cases, this is done as part-time study while the person is teaching or working in the school. Some of the university programs are based on a peer-assisted leadership model, in which part of the training is done by shadowing and being mentored by the senior school principal.

Local education authorities, with the advice and counsel of the teachers, select principals. Principal evaluation, like teacher evaluation, is handled differently in each municipality. In some cases, there is a personal, results-based contract between the principal and the municipality, in which the outcomes and expected results of the principal's work are defined. These contractual outcomes might include qualitative goals like renewed curriculum for the school, an agreed-upon program for preventing bullying, or improved collaboration between the school and

> Most analysts observe that excellent teachers play a critical role in Finland's outstanding educational performance.

community. Quantitative targets might include reducing the number of early school leavers, increasing participation of teachers in professional development, or achieving budget implementation targets. As mentioned above, formal external teacher or leader evaluations do not exist in Finland. Consequently, value-added methods to measure teacher or leader effectiveness are alien to the Finnish education system.

But, as Andy Hargreaves and colleagues concluded in a recent analysis of leadership development in Finland:

> Leadership currently contributes to Finnish high performance not by concentrating or perseverating on performance outcomes, particularly measurable ones, but by paying attention to the conditions, processes, and goals that produce high performance—a common mission; a broad but unobtrusive steering system; strong municipal leadership with lots of local investment in curriculum and educational development; teachers who already are qualified and capable at the point of entry; informal cooperation and distributed leadership; principals who stay close to the classroom, their colleagues, and the culture of teaching; and (from the principal's standpoint) being first among a society of equals in the practical and improvisational practice of school-based improvement. (Hargreaves, Halasz, & Pont, 2008, p. 93)

LESSONS FROM FINLAND'S SUCCESS

No single factor can explain Finland's outstanding educational performance. However, most analysts observe that excellent teachers play a critical role. Certain Finnish practices contribute to a strong teacher workforce:

- Rigorous research-based and practice-oriented teacher education programs that prepare teachers in content, pedagogy, and educational theory, as well as the capacity to do their own research, and that include fieldwork mentored by expert veterans
- Significant financial support for teacher education, professional development, reasonable and equitable salaries, and working conditions that enable lateral professional learning and building social capital in schools
- The creation of a respected profession in which teachers have considerable authority and autonomy, including responsibility for curriculum design and student assessment, which engages them in the ongoing analysis and refinement of practice.

Teachers' capacity to teach in classrooms and work collaboratively in professional communities has been built systematically through academic teacher education. A smart strategy is to invest in quality at the point of entry into teacher education. The Finnish example suggests that a critical condition for attracting the most able young people is that teaching is an independent and respected profession rather than just a technical implementation of externally mandated standards and tests. Teachers' strong competence and preparedness creates the prerequisite for the professional autonomy that makes teaching a valued career.

> A smart strategy is to invest in quality at the point of entry into teacher education.

CHAPTER 4

Systems for Teacher and Leadership Effectiveness and Quality

Ontario, Canada

Barry Pervin
Carol Campbell

In Canada, education is the responsibility of each province or territory. Ontario is Canada's largest and most diverse province. The Ontario publicly funded education system is overseen by the provincial government through the Ontario Ministry of Education. In 2012–2013 there were 2,031,205 students attending a total of 4,981 schools in four publicly funded school systems (English public, English Catholic, French public, and French Catholic). Ontario receives more than half of all newcomers (including immigrants and refugees) into Canada and also has more than half of Canada's "visible minorities" (those who are non-White)—a population that is growing more than four times faster than the general population. Currently, 27% of Ontario students were born outside Canada, with 20% self-identifying as members of a visible minority, and 4.5% of Ontario schoolchildren are French speaking. Approximately 115,500 full-time equivalent teachers, 7,300 school administrators, and 4,400 early childhood educators are employed in Ontario's 72 district school boards (60 English and 12 French), which range widely in size, from a few hundred students in remote rural areas to 250,000 students in the Toronto District School Board. The public education system is generally held in high regard, with 95% of all students attending publicly funded schools (Ontario Ministry of Education, 2013a).

GOVERNMENT PRIORITIES

For about a decade, beginning in the early 1990s, the education system in Ontario was characterized by significant labor disruption, public dissatisfaction, and poor morale leading to high turnover among teachers. In 2004 a new provincial government set an ambitious agenda for education, recognizing that a focused and sustained commitment to education and teaching are key to a strong and prosperous society. The government identified three core priorities to drive its education reform agenda forward:

1. Increased student achievement
2. Reduced gaps in achievement for students
3. Increased public confidence in publicly funded education

Specifically, the Ontario government committed to having 75% of students achieving at the provincial standard (Level 3: or a B grade) in reading, writing, and mathematics in the 6th grade (age 12) and a secondary school graduation rate of 85% of students. As of 2012–2013, these goals were close to being met:

- 71% of students overall achieved the provincial standard of Level 3 or above, compared to 54% in 2003—an increase of 17 percentage points.
- 83% of students graduated from high school within 5 years, compared to 68% in 2004—an increase of 15 percentage points.

The defining feature of Ontario's successful approach to education reform is professional capacity building—at the provincial, district school board, school, and classroom levels—with a focus on results.

> The defining feature of Ontario's successful approach to education reform is professional capacity building.

To support this capacity building, the Ontario Ministry of Education has taken two major steps:

- Created the Literacy and Numeracy Secretariat (LNS) and the Student Success/Learning to 18 Branch to support secondary school student success, now coordinated within the Student Achievement Division
- Made major investments in personnel and resources:
  - ➤ Student achievement officers

➤ Student success leaders

➤ Additional primary and specialist teachers

➤ Professional learning institutes, webinars, instructional guides

➤ Finely tuned strategies that are developed and disseminated to teachers (e.g., Ontario Focused Intervention Partnerships) to help improve teaching and learning in Ontario schools

The ministry has also developed a range of supporting conditions to improve student outcomes, including teacher and leadership development frameworks and peace and stability in labor relations.

Building on the work and progress of the past decade, the ministry recently conducted extensive consultations to develop a renewed vision for Ontario's public education system. The resulting vision, *Achieving Excellence* (Ontario Ministry of Education, 2014), commits to further deepening and expanding educational improvements and equity through four key goals:

- *Achieving Excellence:* Children and students of all ages will achieve high levels of academic performance, acquire valuable skills, and demonstrate good citizenship. Educators will be supported in learning continually and will be recognized as among the best in the world.
- *Ensuring Equity:* All children and students will be inspired to reach their full potential, with access to rich learning experiences that begin at birth and continue into adulthood.
- *Promoting Well-Being:* All children and students will develop enhanced mental and physical health, a positive sense of self and belonging, and the skills to make positive choices.
- *Enhancing Public Confidence:* Ontarians will continue to have confidence in a publicly funded education system that helps develop new generations of confident, capable, and caring citizens.

TEACHER EFFECTIVENESS AND QUALITY: FROM TEACHER TESTING TO TEACHER DEVELOPMENT

The Ontario Ministry of Education recognizes teachers as the single most important factor in the improvement of student achievement, and teacher professional development as the single most important factor in the improvement of teacher quality. This is supported by research that suggests that what teachers know and are able to do is crucial to student learning (Darling-Hammond & Sykes, 1999; Fullan, Hill, & Crevola, 2006; Wilson, Floden, & Ferrini-Mundy, 2001).

In 1997 the Ontario College of Teachers (OCT) was established to regulate the teaching profession in the public interest. (For more information on OCT, see their website at www.oct.ca/.) The college licenses all teachers in Ontario's publicly funded school system, sets standards of practice and conduct for the profession, and investigates complaints against teachers from the public. Self-regulation of the teaching profession encourages a climate of respect and recognition for teachers and raises the profile of teachers with the public.

Ontario has explored a number of different approaches to improve student achievement through teacher development, including a teacher-testing program from 2001 to 2004. The teacher-testing program comprised an entry to the profession test, a recertification program every 5 years, and a teacher evaluation program. The prescriptive nature of the testing program did not encourage teachers to be actively and meaningfully engaged in either their own learning or their students' learning, and was considered punitive and controlling by the profession.

Since 2004, the Ministry of Education has advanced an approach based on respect and professionalism for teachers, teaching practice, and teacher development. A defining feature is a commitment to collective capacity building at all levels of the education system. To create a sense of common purpose and cooperation among education stakeholders, the ministry initiated the Working Table on Teacher Development, an ongoing advisory body intended to provide an effective vehicle for policymakers, teachers, school boards, and teacher labor groups to share different perspectives. The work of the Teacher Development Table led to the creation of a number of innovative teacher development programs for new and experienced teachers, including the New Teacher Induction Program (NTIP), Teacher Performance Appraisal, and the Teacher Learning and Leadership Program (TLLP) (see Figure 4.1).

TEACHER RECRUITMENT

School boards are responsible for the hiring and appointment of teachers to Ontario schools in the public system. Teachers apply to schools of their choice and are assigned to positions based on the program needs of the school and the safety and well-being of students, as well as their own qualifications and seniority. Principals generally make these assignment decisions. Some school boards also have staffing committees, consisting of school and school board staff and representatives of teachers' federations to assist in making staffing decisions.

All teachers in the public system must be members of the Ontario Teachers' Federation and one of its teachers' union affiliates, and all school boards are responsible for negotiating local collective agreements with the federations.

Ontario's employment market is now characterized by an oversupply of trained teachers in most subject areas, especially in elementary schools. Even though the oversupply means that it now takes the average new teacher longer to secure a permanent full-time contract, surveys of teachers beginning their careers in Ontario schools reveal a high level of professional satisfaction and an eagerness to stay in the field.

> Surveys of teachers beginning their careers in Ontario reveal a high level of professional satisfaction and an eagerness to stay in the field.

TEACHER PREPARATION, CONTINUING PROFESSIONAL DEVELOPMENT, AND CAPACITY BUILDING

Teacher preparation and professional development in Ontario are based on a framework of experience, training, professional learning, and appraisal over the stages of a teacher's career ranging across preservice, new teacher, experienced teacher, and teacher leadership stages, as outlined in Figure 4.1. The framework is based on the idea that effective and life-long teacher development depends on teachers taking ownership of their learning and having the capacity to develop and renew themselves.

Initial Teacher Education

Before 2015, Ontario teachers had to complete a minimum of 3 or 4 years of undergraduate study and further teacher preservice education at a faculty of education at an Ontario university before becoming certified with the Ontario College of Teachers (OCT). Initial teacher education is only available via accredited university faculties of education. In order to be accredited, preservice programs were required to satisfy 15 broad requirements outlined in O. Reg. 347/02 (Accreditation of Teacher Education Programs) under the Ontario College of Teachers Act of 1996.

Figure 4.1. Teacher Development in Ontario

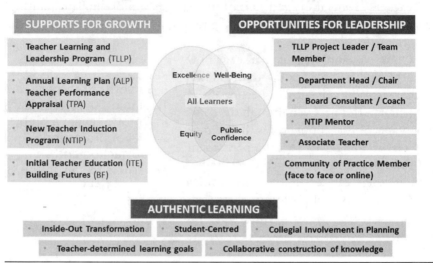

Teaching Policy and Standards Branch
(Leadership and Learning Environment Division, EDU)

Fostering Teacher Growth & Development

SUPPORTS FOR GROWTH

- Teacher Learning and Leadership Program (TLLP)
- Annual Learning Plan (ALP)
- Teacher Performance Appraisal (TPA)
- New Teacher Induction Program (NTIP)
- Initial Teacher Education (ITE)
- Building Futures (BF)

Excellence Well-Being

All Learners

Equity Public Confidence

OPPORTUNITIES FOR LEADERSHIP

- TLLP Project Leader / Team Member
- Department Head / Chair
- Board Consultant / Coach
- NTIP Mentor
- Associate Teacher
- Community of Practice Member (face to face or online)

AUTHENTIC LEARNING

- Inside-Out Transformation
- Student-Centred
- Collegial Involvement in Planning
- Teacher-determined learning goals
- Collaborative construction of knowledge

Source: Teaching and Policy Standards Branch, Ontario Ministry of Education © Queen's Printer for Ontario, 2015. Reproduced with permission.

The general model of preservice teacher education has been 1 year of university study (consecutive to or concurrent with an undergraduate degree) including a minimum of 40 days of practicum experience in a host school with an identified associate teacher.

However, in 2013 the provincial government announced major changes to initial teacher education in Ontario. Effective from 2015 onwards, the length of the preservice program is to double to a 4-semester, 2-year university program, with a minimum of 80 days of practicum experience. The new program is also intended to include an enhanced focus on preparing teachers for working with, and appreciating, student and community diversity, students identified as having special needs, issues of mental health for young people, and the integration of technology into teaching practices. Alongside the extension of the program, there has also been a reduction in government funding to university providers for teacher

> The new program for preservice teachers is intended to focus on diversity, special needs, mental health for young people, and the integration of technology.

education places from 9,000 funded places (as of 2013) to 4,500 funded places from 2015 onwards. In part, the reduction in places is associated with an oversupply of qualified teachers compared to available teaching positions in Ontario. Nevertheless, large numbers of students continue to apply to teacher education, suggesting that the future competitiveness of successful entry to teacher education may increase substantially.

In addition to university preparation, since 2004, the Ministry of Education has delivered the Building Futures program (see www.edu. gov.on.ca/eng/teachers/buildingfutures/) to assist teacher candidates in understanding key government education priorities as they make the transition from university to the school classroom. Candidates receive information and resources about education priorities and effective teaching strategies through a series of workshops by experienced educators.

New Teacher Induction Program (NTIP)

The New Teacher Induction Program (NTIP; see www.edu.gov.on.ca/eng/teacher/induction.html) is mandatory for new teachers employed on a permanent contract or long-term occasional (assignment for minimum of 97 days) position in Ontario's public school system. The NTIP provides a range of supports, including orientation, mentoring for the 1st year (and potential for mentoring in the 2nd year), and professional development, and includes two performance appraisals by the school principal and a notation on the teaching certificate indicating successful completion of the program. The professional development focuses on key areas of need identified by new teachers, including classroom management, communication with parents, and assessment and evaluation. NTIP mentors are generally colleagues in the new teachers' school. Becoming a mentor is voluntary, although criteria for selection of mentors and their training are specified by the Ministry of Education.

According to data collected by the OCT in 2012, nearly all teachers comply with the requirement to participate in the program; 92% of 1st-year teachers in regular teaching positions, as well as 25% of those in first-time long-term occasional positions, reporting being involved in NTIP. Similarly, 81% of regular appointees in 2nd year and 37% of long-term occasional teachers reported that they are in the NTIP. Mentors and other experienced teachers involved in the NTIP received positive evaluations from participating new teachers. The majority (90%) of new teachers rated the support they received for practical day-to-day teaching responsibilities as "very helpful" or "helpful" (OCT, 2012).

Teacher Appraisal and Evaluation

The Teacher Performance Appraisal (TPA) system (see www.edu.gov.
on.ca/eng/teacher/appraise.html), developed in collaboration with key
education stakeholders, provides teachers with meaningful appraisals that
encourage professional learning and growth. The appraisal process was
revised in 2004 in light of teacher and administrator dissatisfaction with
the earlier system, reducing the frequency of
evaluations and the number of evaluation ratings while focusing more pointedly on teacher
development and identifying opportunities for
additional support where required. Each teacher is appraised every 5 years by his or her school
principal based on competencies that reflect
standards of practice set out by OCT, including
standards of professional practice and ethical standards for the teaching
profession (OCT, 2014).

> The appraisal
> process was revised
> in light of teacher
> and administrator
> dissatisfaction.

As part of the appraisal process, experienced teachers must complete
an Annual Learning Plan (ALP) each year, outlining their plan for professional growth. Developing, maintaining, and updating the ALP provides
teachers and principals with an opportunity to collaborate and to engage
in discussion about teachers' performance, growth strategies, and professional learning specific to their needs. Pilot approaches to developing collaborative ALPs for groups of teachers, for example by division or grade
or school, over a multiyear process are currently under way as an approach to further facilitate collaborative learning
focused on priority goals.

> An Annual
> Learning Plan (ALP)
> provides teachers
> and principals with
> an opportunity to
> collaborate.

Although the performance appraisal process for new and experienced teachers focuses
on teacher growth and development, there are
a small number of cases where continued unsatisfactory performance results in the termination
of a teacher's employment.

Teacher Learning and Leadership Program

Experienced teachers may apply to participate in the Teacher Learning
and Leadership Program (TLLP; see www.edu.gov.on.ca/eng/teacher/
tllp.html) in order to innovate, apply, model, and share best practices
with other teachers through self-directed, job-embedded professional
development projects, which are funded by the Ministry of Education

working in partnership with the Ontario Teachers' Federation. Projects explore a wide range of innovative practices; most common are projects focusing on differentiating instruction for students' needs, integrating technology and pedagogy to engage students, literacy, and development of professional learning communities.

Teachers involved in the TLLP become part of a provincial network of professional learning where their knowledge and learning is shared with other teachers within and outside their boards. Information about completed projects is made available provincewide through a provincial Sharing the Learning Summit and online sharing of resources and experiences (see the Mentoring Moments Ning at mentoringmoments.ning.com). The development of resources and materials from TLLP projects, such as lesson plans, enhances sharing of practice with other teachers. Sharing is also supported through teachers' contributing to professional learning activities and through online and social media. Research about the TLLP has identified considerable benefits for experienced teachers participating in teacher-led projects and professional learning, including improvements in professional knowledge and understanding, in instructional practices, and in self-efficacy and leadership skills (Campbell, Lieberman, & Yashkina, 2013a, 2013b).

> Knowledge and learning is shared through a provincial Sharing the Learning Summit and online sharing of resources.

Additional Qualifications

More than 35,000 teachers take Additional Qualifications (AQ) programs every year to upgrade their qualifications and enhance their practice. AQ programs are offered by Ontario faculties of education and other organizations and are accredited by OCT. These programs are voluntary, taken on a teacher's own personal time (e.g., during the summer), and paid for by the teacher (up to C$1,000 per program). On average, teachers spend over C$25 million of their own money on AQ programs each year in total. Teachers obtain AQs in order to develop greater knowledge and expertise in particular areas of study and to move up the salary grid. The most popular AQs are special education, English as a second language, and French as a second language.

The Ministry of Education and the Ontario Teachers' Federation also sponsor summer institutes for teachers to enhance their knowledge and skills in a range of provincial priority areas. These summer institutes are very well attended and are offered at minimal cost to teachers.

Teacher Recognition and Reward

Teachers' salaries in Ontario range from C$42,000 to C$92,000 within a 12-year salary grid. The grid provides for increases in salaries based on qualifications and experience. Teachers can move between salary categories by completing a specific number of AQ programs. Teachers can receive additional remuneration for responsibilities beyond regular classroom duties (e.g., acting as a department head). Teachers may also take on other roles in their schools, such as volunteering for extracurricular activities or acting as mentors for new teachers, which are not associated with additional remuneration.

The government successfully facilitated a process in 2005 and 2009 to implement a provincial bargaining framework to establish 4-year collective agreements across Ontario and to avoid labor disruption. This has promoted peace and stability throughout the publicly funded school system. In 2012, however, difficulties in making 4-year collective agreements with all unions and changes by the government to the bargaining process resulted in disputes. In 2014, Bill 122, the School Boards Collective Bargaining Act, was passed by the government to formalize a two-tier bargaining system going forward with major financial issues to be centrally bargained between representatives of the provincial government, school boards, and teachers' unions, while local matters will continue to be negotiated between individual school boards and the unions that hold bargaining rights in that particular jurisdiction.

> Salaries in Ontario range from C$42,000 to C$92,000 within a 12-year salary grid.

LEADERSHIP EFFECTIVENESS

The Ministry of Education considers school leaders to be instructional leaders and school leadership to be a key supporting condition in the achievement of its education priorities. In 2005 the ministry released a paper on the role of the principal called *Leading Education: New Supports for Principals and Vice-Principals in Ontario Publicly Funded Schools* (see www.edu.gov.on.ca/eng/general/elemsec/partnership/leadingEducation.html), outlining five goals:

1. Ensure that conditions exist that permit principals to perform their key function as the "instructional leader"
2. Provide high-quality training

3. Increase input that principals and vice principals have within the education system
4. Improve respect and security
5. Better define the role, powers, and responsibilities

Principal Preparation

All principals and vice principals must attain principals' qualifications by completing the Principals' Qualification Program (PQP). The program is accredited by OCT and consists of two parts, each totalling 125 hours, plus a practicum. The program is provided by faculties of education and by principals' associations. The PQP is structured around the Ontario Leadership Framework. In addition to completing the PQP, principals must have an undergraduate degree, 5 years of classroom experience, qualifications in three divisions of the school system, and a master's or double-subject specialist degree.

The Ontario Leadership Strategy and Leadership Framework

The ministry's extensive Ontario Leadership Strategy (OLS; see www.edu.gov. on.ca/eng/policyfunding/leadership/ index.html) is a comprehensive plan of action designed to support student achievement and well-being by attracting and developing skilled and passionate school and system leaders. The theory of action driving the OLS is that significant progress toward the province's three core education priorities can be accomplished by the following steps:

> Principals must have an undergraduate degree, 5 years of classroom experience, qualifications in three divisions of the school system, and a master's or double-subject specialist degree.

- Directly improving the quality of school and district leadership
- Supporting and adding value to efforts of others responsible for leadership development
- Working to improve conditions for teaching and learning in schools and classrooms

The OLS is underpinned and informed by a research-based framework for leadership development (see Figure 4.2).

The Ontario Leadership Framework was first introduced in 2006. It identifies effective leadership practices in five domains:

1. Setting directions
2. Building relationships and developing people
3. Developing the organization
4. Leading the instructional program
5. Securing accountability

The Leadership Framework is a nonmandated tool to guide leadership practice. Its purpose is to promote a common language that fosters an understanding of leadership and what it means to be a school and system leader, to make explicit the connections between leaders' influence and the quality of teaching and learning, and to guide the design and implementation of professional learning and development of school and system leaders. The Framework contains core leadership practices to inform vice principals and principals in schools and supervisory officers in school districts.

The Ontario Leadership Framework was updated, refined, and revised in 2013 to ensure that the practices within each domain took account of the latest research. Changes included:

- Revised leadership practices for school and system leaders
- Introduction of the District Effectiveness Framework
- More explicit connections to the ministry's K–12 School Effectiveness Framework

In addition, a new category of personal leadership resources was introduced for the domains of:

- *Cognitive resources:* problem-solving expertise, and knowledge about school and classroom conditions with direct effects on student learning
- *Social resources:* perceiving emotions, managing emotions, and acting in emotionally appropriate ways
- *Psychological resources:* optimism, self-efficacy, and resilience (Leithwood, 2012).

Leadership Recruitment, Recognition, and Retention

School boards decide on the placement of principals in specific schools by looking at the talent pool of candidates, the needs of their schools, and the career preferences of their current leaders where possible, taking into account advice from school councils. Some factors may serve as deterrents for teachers to become vice principals or principals, including a

Figure 4.2. Ontario Leadership Strategy and Framework

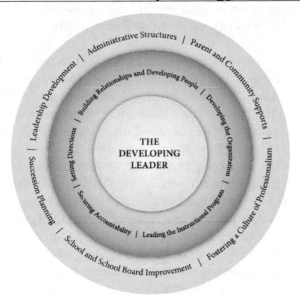

Source: Leadership Development and School Board Governance Branch, Ontario Ministry of Education © Queen's Printer for Ontario, 2015. Reproduced with permission.

negligible salary increase, if any, and the fact that teachers must leave the protection of their federation or union in order to take on the new role. Still, most school leaders indicate that they like their jobs, and very few leave prior to the average retirement age.

Through the Ontario Leadership Strategy, each school district in Ontario is provided with funding and support to develop and implement a Board Leadership Development Strategy (BLDS; see www.edu.gov. on.ca/eng/policyfunding/leadership/BLDSQuickFacts.pdf), which focuses on school and system leaders and all those within the district who aspire to take on leadership roles, whether on the academic or business side of the organization. The BLDS focuses on four key areas:

- *Recruiting and selecting leaders* through structured and innovative succession planning
- *Placing and transferring leaders* in ways that sustain school and system improvement
- *Developing leaders* through mentoring, performance appraisal, and differentiated learning opportunities that meet the needs of leaders in diverse contexts and at various stages of their careers

- *Coordinating support for leaders* to buffer them from distractions, make information easily accessible, and assist them in building coherence across different initiatives

Much of the early emphasis of the Ontario Leadership Strategy was on getting infrastructures and processes in place to ensure that leadership development could happen in all parts of the province. Evidence collected through the first 4 years (2008–2012) confirmed that infrastructure has been built within and across districts. Since 2012, the focus has moved from developing infrastructures to measuring the impact of their Board Leadership Development Strategies as districts engage in a cyclical process of assessing impact, setting high-quality goals, implementing evidence-based strategies, and monitoring the implementation of those strategies. Such a well-planned and well-executed BLDS can help to build coherence in the achievement of goals identified in a Board Improvement Plan for Student Achievement developed by each school district.

In 2012 the ministry developed the BLDS Impact Assessment and Planning Tool and asked districts to self-assess their progress using it. Districts are becoming more adept at gathering and using data to measure the impact of their BLDS and to respond by setting goals and targeting supports in areas that will have the greatest impact and where the need is greatest. Senior leaders are using leadership development strategies to change and develop the culture of their organizations. More often now, leadership goals are embedded in the overall school district's strategic plan and connected to student achievement goals.

Principal Mentoring

All principals and vice principals are offered mentoring for their first 2 years in each role (see www.edu.gov.on.ca/eng/policyfunding/leadership/mentoring.html), funded by the ministry and delivered by school boards according to ministry guidelines. Features of the mentoring program include training for mentors, a learning plan outlining how the mentor and mentee will work together, and a transparent matching and exit process to ensure a good fit between mentor and mentee.

Principal Performance Appraisal

All principals and vice principals are appraised every 5 years through the Principal Performance Appraisal (PPA) process summarized in Figure 4.3 (Ontario Ministry of Education, 2013b). As part of the appraisal process,

All principals and vice principals are offered mentoring for their first 2 years.

principals, in consultation with their supervisors, must set a few challenging yet achievable goals based on ministry, school board, school, community, and personal priorities, plus taking account of leadership practices in the Ontario Leadership Framework, and develop strategies to meet these goals. At the end of the appraisal year, principals are appraised according to the progress they have made in meeting their goals. If this is unsatisfactory, a process is followed that includes an improvement plan, time for improvement, and the offering of supports. If insufficient improvement is made, the board has the authority to demote, transfer, or terminate employment. An annual growth plan—connected to the Ontario Leadership Framework—outlines the activities that the principal will engage in to support the performance plan.

CAPACITY BUILDING THROUGH JOB-EMBEDDED PROFESSIONAL LEARNING AND COLLABORATIVE PRACTICE

The Ministry of Education's capacity-building strategies to support effective leadership, teaching, and student learning are multifaceted. For example, teachers and principals have 6 professional activity days every school year to work with one another on activities related to key ministry priorities and local school and school board needs.

The ministry also fosters capacity building and collaboration by sharing information about existing and emerging successful practices. Through the Schools on the Move strategy (see www.edu.gov.on.ca/eng/literacynumeracy/schoolMove.html), for example, the ministry highlighted elementary schools that have made substantial and sustained gains in student achievement, often in challenging contexts, and provides information to other schools about the practices that have contributed to their success. The ministry also develops and disseminates webcasts and online resources, including videos of effective practices from Ontario's classrooms, to support schools in their efforts to build capacity (Curriculum Services Canada, 2013).

The Ontario Literacy and Numeracy strategies have placed a strong emphasis on the development of improvements in instructional practices in elementary schools, for example, through a current range of

The Ontario Literacy and Numeracy strategies have placed a strong emphasis on the development of improvements in instructional practices.

Figure 4.3. Principal Performance Appraisal Process

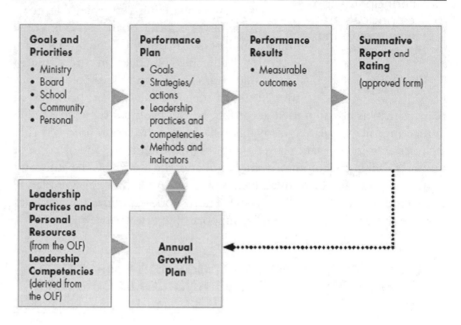

Source: Ontario Ministry of Education © Queen's Printer for Ontario, 2013. Reproduced with permission. From *Principal/vice-principal performance appraisal: Technical requirements manual, 2013* (p. 12) (Available atwww.edu.gov.on.ca/eng/policyfunding/leadership/PPA_Manual.pdf).

collaborative inquiry initiatives (see www.edu.gov.on.ca/eng/literacynu-meracy/collaborative.html) to support educators' professional learning and improved practices in order to support and engage students' learning. For secondary schools, the Student Success strategy (see www.edu.gov.on.ca/eng/teachers/studentsuccess/strategy.html) focuses on the development of a flexible range of programs and pathways to support high school students to (re)engage in education and graduate from high school.

Building on the work of the literacy and numeracy strategies for elementary schools and Student Success strategies for secondary schools, the ministry has introduced the K–12 School Effectiveness Framework, shown in Figure 4.4, which places aligned planning, actions, and capacity building at the center of the work of all levels of the education system (Ontario Ministry of Education, 2013c). Schools are encouraged to use the School Effectiveness Framework to conduct self-assessments of the school's priorities to inform School Improvement Plans and to monitor progress toward identified goals.

Figure 4.4. K–12 School Effectiveness Framework

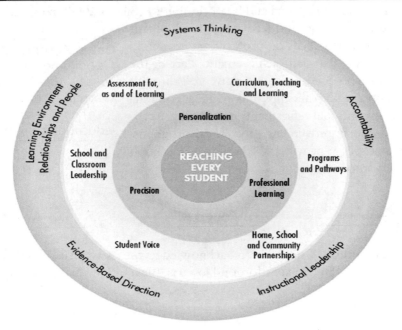

Source: Ontario Ministry of Education © Queen's Printer for Ontario, 2013. Reproduced with permission. From *2013 School Effectiveness Framework: A support for school improvement and student success, K–12* (p. 4) (Available at www.edu.gov.on.ca/eng/literacynumeracy/SEF2013.pdf).

LESSONS LEARNED

Ontario's approach to teacher and leadership effectiveness is building a rich culture of learning across all parts of its diverse education system. Its education reform agenda is based on professional capacity building and has the following characteristics:

- Shared understanding of the importance of setting clear goals for high standards of achievement to enable students of all abilities and backgrounds to achieve their fullest potential
- Respect for teachers as professionals who are committed to developing their practice through collaborative inquiry and differentiated instruction to achieve excellent results for their students
- Supportive instructional leadership from school principals and district leaders within a coherent framework that is focused on the classroom and inspired by students

The Ontario Ministry of Education has made great progress with its education reform agenda and is continuing to collaborate with education partners on teacher and leadership development frameworks that focus on professional growth in the context of student achievement. Part of the Ontario approach is to "learn as we go" through collaborative partnerships involving a commitment to continual refinement, monitoring, adaptation, and improvement of policies, programs, and practices at provincial, school board, school, and classroom levels.

> Ontario's approach is building a rich culture of learning across all parts of its diverse education system.

NOTE

The authors would like to acknowledge the assistance of Rebecca Cossar, Kirsty Henderson, Jordon Douglas, Eleanor Newman, and Laurie Pedwell.

CHAPTER 5

Creating Effective Teachers and Leaders in Singapore

Tan Lay Choo and Linda Darling-Hammond

Our teachers are simply the most important asset we have. Their commitment to excellence, their caring eye, and the passion they put into nurturing their students are what allow us to provide the best possible education to every young Singaporean.

—Mr. Tharman Shammugaratnam, Minister for Education (2007)

CONTEXT

Shortly after Singapore became independent in 1965, its leaders realized that, since the nation had few natural resources, its future would rely on the knowledge and skills of its people. At that time, with relatively few people entering and completing high school, only a small number of people graduated from high school or college, and the nation had few skilled workers. Today, by contrast, about 75% of young people complete postsecondary education in a college or a polytechnic, and nearly all of the remainder receive a vocational degree that prepares them for work, which is increasingly likely to be in a high-tech field in one of the many multinational corporations locating in Singapore (Darling-Hammond, 2010).

> This small nation seeks to ensure that every student has access to strong teaching, an inquiry curriculum, and cutting-edge technology.

This small nation—about the same size as Minnesota—has been steadily building an education system that seeks to ensure that every student has access to strong teaching, an inquiry curriculum, and cutting-edge technology.

A strong teaching force has always been considered critical to the development of a strong education system in Singapore. As early as 1966, the minister for education, Ong Pang Boon, noted,

> Teachers have a heavy responsibility, as the future of every one of us in Singapore is to a large extent determined by what teachers do in the classroom. . . . The Singapore government recognises the worth of teachers and realises that it is essential that we have well-qualified and well-paid teachers to have a good education system. (quoted in Goh & Gopinathan, 2008)

Singapore's education system came to international attention when its students scored first in the world in both mathematics and science on the Trends in International Mathematics and Science Study (TIMSS) assessments in 2003. About 90% of Singapore's students scored above the international median on the TIMSS tests. In 2009, when it first entered the Programme in International Student Assessment (PISA), Singapore also scored near the top of the rankings in mathematics, science, and reading.

These rankings are based on strong achievement for all of the country's students, including the Malay and Tamil minorities, who have been rapidly closing what was once a yawning achievement gap (Dixon, 2005). This accomplishment is even more remarkable given that fewer than half of Singapore's students routinely speak English, the language of the test, at home. Most speak one of the other official national languages of the country—Mandarin, Malay, or Tamil—and some speak one of several dozen other languages or dialects.

These successes are the product of a long-term commitment to developing a high-quality educational system, with each era of reform building on previous efforts, while acknowledging new realities. Current initiatives are an outgrowth of a systemwide reform called Thinking Schools, Learning Nation, launched by former Prime Minister Goh Chok Tong in 1997. The Ministry of Education explains that this initiative was meant to create

> Singapore's students scored first in the world in both mathematics and science on TIMSS in 2003. Singapore also scored near the top of the rankings in mathematics, science, and reading on PISA in 2009.

> . . . a nation of thinking and committed citizens capable of meeting the challenges of the future, and an education system geared to the needs of the 21st century.

Thinking schools will be learning organizations in every sense, constantly challenging assumptions, and seeking better ways of doing things through participation, creativity and innovation. Thinking Schools will be the cradle of thinking students as well as thinking adults and this spirit of learning should accompany our students even after they leave school.

A Learning Nation envisions a national culture and social environment that promotes lifelong learning in our people. The capacity of Singaporeans to continually learn, both for professional development and for personal enrichment, will determine our collective tolerance for change. (Singapore Ministry of Education, 2014, paras. 2–4)

To develop this spirit of creativity and innovation, schools are encouraged to engage both students and teachers in experiential and cooperative learning, action research, scientific investigations, entrepreneurial activities, and discussion and debate. Well-prepared and well-supported teachers and leaders are at the center of these efforts (Ng, 2008).

> To develop creativity and innovation, schools engage both students and teachers in experiential and cooperative learning, action research, scientific investigations, entrepreneurial activities, and discussion and debate.

RECRUITING AND KEEPING TOP CANDIDATES

In Singapore, teacher education is a serious investment throughout the career. Teachers are hired centrally by the Ministry of Education (MOE). To get the best teachers, the MOE recruits from the top one-third of each cohort for a 1-year graduate program or, if they enter earlier, a 4-year undergraduate teacher education program. (Currently, about two-thirds are prepared in the graduate program and one-third are prepared in the undergraduate program.) In either case, candidates are immediately put on the MOE's payroll. When they enter teaching, they earn as much as or more than the average starting salary of fresh graduates with similar qualifications in the job market. Principals sit on the recruitment interview panels. The first assignment for a teacher is based on the manpower needs of the nation's schools. After 2 years, teachers can request a posting to a school of their choice, subject to approval by their principal and the receiving principal. A principal can also identify teachers to be posted to his or her school, subject to agreement from the other principal. In addition, there is a yearly posting exercise in which teachers who have requested a job rotation are centrally posted according to manpower needs.

The attrition rate of teachers is less than 3% annually. This is low compared to other public and private organizations. (By comparison, attrition rates for teachers in the United States range from 6% to 8% annually.) In a recent MOE survey, teachers indicated the following top three reasons for staying in the field: a positive culture with a strong sense of mission; good compensation and rewards benchmarked against market rates; and a wide range of opportunities for professional growth and development.

> Teachers indicate three reasons for staying: a positive culture, good compensation, and opportunities for professional growth.

PREPARING TEACHERS WELL

Teacher education programs were overhauled in 2001 to increase teachers' pedagogical knowledge and skills on top of their content preparation, which includes, even for elementary teachers, a deep mastery of one content area plus preparation for the four major subjects they must teach (English language, mathematics, science, and social studies). Practicum training has been expanded and located in a new "school partnership" model, which engages schools more proactively in supporting trainees (Chuan & Gopinathan, 2005) through stronger, more structured relationships between schools and universities and more purposeful practicum experiences connecting teacher candidates with master teachers.

Growing efforts have been made to engage candidates in the kind of inquiry and reflection in which they are expected to engage their students, so they can teach for independent learning, integrated project work, and innovation. During the course of preparation, there is a focus on learning to use problem-based and inquiry learning, on developing collaboration, and on addressing a range of learning styles in the classroom.

All preservice preparation occurs in the National Institute of Education (NIE), affiliated with Nanyang Technological University (NTU), which prepares more than 2,000 teachers per year. At the NIE, candidates learn to teach in the same way they will be asked to teach. Every student has a laptop, and the entire campus is wireless. The library spaces and a growing number of classrooms are consciously arranged with round tables and groups of three to four chairs so students will have places to share knowledge and

> There is a focus on problem-based and inquiry learning, on developing collaboration, and on addressing a range of learning styles.

collaborate. A comfortable area with sofa and chair arrangements is designed for group work among teachers and principals. The grouping areas are soundproofed with an overhead circular cone so several groups can work together in the same room. NIE classrooms offer access to full technology supports (e.g., video recording and computer hookup; a plasma projection screen), and the wall is a whiteboard for recording ideas.

Candidates have practicum opportunities in classrooms with teachers who have been deemed good models of these practices. The 4-year undergraduate program includes frequent practicum experiences in every year of their training: Candidates spend more than 20 weeks working in the classroom over the course of their preparation. The 1-year graduate program includes a 10-week practicum in a school. The practicum is jointly supervised and assessed by a lecturer from the Institute of Education and a supervising senior teacher in the school. A pass in the practicum is necessary for the award of a diploma (National Institute of Education, 2010).

The institute has been creative in thinking about how to help teachers envision new modes of practice beyond those they see in their student teaching. For example, a model classroom has been constructed at the NIE to give educators a vision of what learning will be like in the future. It includes handheld computers; a coffee bar where students can meet at round tables and work on educational video games; and communications with other students in other countries who are working on solving a problem together (e.g., identifying a virus that is spreading, collecting data, running tests, accessing information over the Internet), working on the subway while tracking friends, working at home where interactive technology connects families and friends in communication, and working in a classroom that, again, features round tables surrounded by chairs and in which students are engaged in more inquiry and problem solving. These settings are used as the site for learning new teaching strategies.

> Classrooms offer access to full technology supports (e.g., plasma projection screen), and whiteboard.

The NIE conducts its own evaluation of the preservice courses and gathers feedback from the new teachers on the effectiveness of these courses in teacher preparation. The information is used internally by the NIE to make program improvements.

Current initiatives in preservice preparation of teachers include the use of videos of teaching (both their own and that of others who are expert teachers) to support teachers' analysis of practice and to strengthen the theory-practice connection. In addition, preparation emphasizes the integration of pedagogies for teaching 21st-century skills, preparing teachers for formative assessment and performance assessments, and a new e-portfolio providing evidence of a student teacher's learning and reflections over time to support development and confirm the attainment of teaching competencies.

ONGOING PROFESSIONAL LEARNING FOR TEACHERS

Support for Beginning Teachers

Beginning teachers are equipped with the basic theories and practical skills to teach. However, the preservice program may not adequately prepare them in the whole repertoire of skills and competencies needed to be effective teachers. After initial preparation, novice teachers are not just left to sink or swim. Following preservice preparation, beginning teachers are mentored and coached by senior teachers for 2 years. Expert teachers, trained by the NIE as mentors, are given released time to help beginners learn their craft. During the structured mentoring period, beginning teachers also attend courses in classroom management, counseling, reflective practices, and assessment offered by the NIE and the MOE. During this period, novices are given a lighter workload (i.e., two-thirds that of a more experienced teacher) to help them ease into the teaching profession. These 2 years serve as an extended practicum, and their performance is used to determine their confirmation in the service. (Confirmation is analogous to having tenure; teachers do not need to be recertified or licensed after confirmation.)

> Expert teachers are given released time to help beginners learn their craft.

Continual Professional Learning

On average, the government pays for 100 hours of professional development each year for all teachers. There is a wide range of professional development courses and conferences/seminars. Teachers can also take professional development leaves and sabbaticals to enhance their skills. The MOE has just established a new teachers' academy to support professional development opportunities across schools. The academy serves to facilitate teacher-initiated and teacher-led learning

> Novices are given a lighter workload to help them ease into the teaching profession.

opportunities for the teaching fraternity organized around subject chapters and special interest groups.

Teachers have approximately 20 hours of timetabled teaching periods per week out of a work week of approximately 40 hours. Teachers can make use of their nonteaching hours to work with other teachers on lesson preparation, visit other classrooms to study teaching, or engage in professional discussions and meetings with teachers from their school or their cluster.

> **Teachers have approximately 20 hours of timetabled teaching periods per week.**

The MOE and the NIE have been training teachers to undertake action research projects in the classroom so they can examine teaching and learning problems and find solutions that can be disseminated to others. To support school-based learning, senior and master teachers are appointed to lead the coaching and development of the teachers in each school. The MOE conducts regular surveys to gather feedback from teachers. The relevant findings concerning inservice training are taken up by both the MOE and the NIE for continual improvement.

Among Singapore's many investments in teacher professional learning in 1998 was the Teachers Network, established by the MOE as part of the Thinking Schools initiative. The Teachers Network was created to serve as a catalyst and support for teacher-initiated development through sharing, collaboration, and reflection. It has sponsored learning circles, teacher-led workshops, conferences, and a well-being program, as well as a website and publications series for sharing knowledge (Tripp, 2004).

In a *learning circle*, four to ten teachers and a facilitator collaboratively identify and solve common problems chosen by the participating teachers using discussions and action research. The learning circles generally meet for eight 2-hour sessions over a period of 4 to 12 months. Professional development officers, who are supported by the national university, conduct an initial whole-school training program on the key processes of reflection, dialogue, and action research. They also run a more extended program to train teachers as learning circle facilitators and mentor facilitators in the field. A major part of the facilitator's role is to encourage the teachers to act as co-learners and critical friends so they feel safe to take the risks of sharing their assumptions and personal theories, experimenting with new ideas and practices, and sharing their successes and problems. Discussing problems and possible solutions in learning circles fosters a sense of collegiality among teachers and encourages teachers to be reflective practitioners. Learning circles allow teachers to feel that they are producing knowledge, not just disseminating received knowledge.

Teacher-led workshops provide teachers an opportunity to present their ideas and work with their colleagues in a collegial atmosphere where everyone, including the presenter, is a co-learner and critical friend. Each workshop is jointly planned with a Teachers Network professional development officer to ensure that everyone will be a co-learner in the workshop. The presenters first prepare an outline of their workshop, then the professional development officer helps the presenters surface their tacit knowledge and assumptions and trains them in facilitation so they do not present as an expert with all the answers, but share and discuss the challenges they face in the classroom. The process is time-consuming, but almost all teacher-presenters find that it leads to them grow professionally.

> Learning circle facilitators encourage the teachers to act as co-learners and critical friends so they feel safe.

Eventually, the Academy of Singapore Teachers (AST) was set up to take over the functions of the Teachers Network with expanded responsibilities. While the Teachers Network was a department under the Ministry of Education, the AST is governed by a Teachers Council headed by the director-general of education. It aims to further deepen professional practice by growing professional learning communities who collaborate and share their practices, so that best practices of master, lead, and senior teachers are scalable to more classrooms across the nation.

The goal of a teacher-led culture of professional collaboration and learning is pursued through workshops and seminars, as well as the establishment of subject-specific professional learning communities supported by Subject Chapters at the AST. To facilitate sharing of teaching resources, the AST also manages an online portal for teachers to share their teaching resources and for those who download these resources to provide comments and feedback (see the AST website at www. academyofsingaporeteachers.moe.gov.sg/).

> A teacher-led culture of professional collaboration is pursued through workshops and seminars.

CAREER DEVELOPMENT AND LEADERSHIP

Career development is a constant concern in Singapore schools. Principals, cluster superintendents (each of whom oversees a network of about a dozen schools), and MOE senior management all pay attention to teachers' talents and potentials to support promotions and tap teachers for a variety of leadership roles.

Teacher performance is evaluated through a performance management process using the Enhanced Performance Management System (EPMS). The EPMS is a competency-based performance management system that spells out the knowledge, skills, competencies, and attitudes expected at each stage of the career and within each of three career tracks: the teaching track, which extends through levels of senior, lead, and master teachers; the specialist track, which includes roles like curriculum specialist, educational psychologist, and guidance counselor; and the leadership track, which progresses through roles like department head, vice principal, principal, superintendent, and divisional heads and directors (see Figure 5.1). These opportunities bring recognition, extra compensation, and new challenges that keep teaching exciting.

Teachers are assessed based on their contributions to the holistic development of students (i.e., quality of students' learning, pastoral care and well-being of students, cocurricular activities, and collaboration with parents). The evaluation takes into consideration both processes and outcomes in academic as well as nonacademic domains. All teachers are assessed yearly using the EPMS. They are expected to have a minimum of two one-on-one work review sessions with their head of department, who is their immediate supervisor. The final assessment is reviewed and endorsed by the school principal. Outcomes include classroom success of students, but external exams occur only in 6th and 10th grades, so outside test scores are not generally part of the evaluation process.

> Opportunities bring recognition, extra compensation, and new challenges that keep teaching exciting.

Annual evaluations are used to establish a performance bonus set by the principal for each teacher, as well as to flag struggling teachers for additional assistance or potential dismissal (a very tiny number), and to flag successful teachers for potential promotions. In considering teachers for promotion or progression along each of the three career tracks, their performance evaluations in the last 3 years are taken into consideration. There is flexibility of lateral movements across the three career tracks.

> Teachers are assessed based on the holistic development of students.

As teachers are promoted and selected into these kinds of roles, they receive free courses of study through the MOE at the NIE, sometimes

Figure 5.1. Career Tracks for Teachers

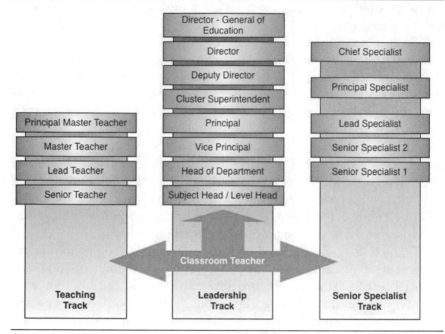

Source: Reproduced with permission of Academy of Singapore Teachers, Ministry of Education, Singapore.

while they are still teaching and other times while taking a sabbatical from their jobs. Teachers who take on higher levels of responsibility, such as head of department or principal, will eventually be promoted to a higher pay scale commensurate with their respective roles and responsibilities. Figure 5.1 illustrates that a teacher has the opportunity to progress to a promotional grade and pay scale equivalent to that of a school principal if they reach the pinnacle of the master teacher track. Similarly, a specialist can progress to as high a promotional grade as that of a director.

Advancement Along the Teaching Track

Those aspiring to advance within the teaching track must meet accreditation standards for the positions. These standards are assessed through a professional portfolio, which includes the following documents:

- A personal statement on taking up the higher appointment
- A summary of evidence satisfying each accreditation standard
- Supporting data to substantiate the evidence (e.g., lesson plans, presentations, and so on)

The accreditation standards build on the evaluation criteria used to evaluate teaching (holistic development of pupils through quality learning, pastoral care and well-being, and cocurricular activities), adding progressively broader criteria at each career level. These include such things as contributions to the school, cluster, zone, and nation; collaboration and networking; and contributions to a culture of professionalism, ethos, and standards.

Advancement Along the Specialist Track

The senior specialist track aims to develop a strong core of officers in the MOE with deep knowledge and skills in areas such as curriculum, planning, educational programs, and educational technology. These specialists are supported in pursuing advanced graduate study (master's and doctorate degrees), and they work in clusters that help guide policy and practice for curriculum and assessment, educational psychology and guidance, and educational research and measurement.

> The senior specialist track aims to develop a strong core of officers with deep knowledge and skills.

Advancement Along the Leadership Track

Inasmuch as leadership is seen as a key enabler for strong schools, much attention and resources are given to identify and groom school leaders. Teachers with leadership potential are identified early and groomed for leadership positions. They progress from teacher to subject head, head of department, vice principal, and then principal.

Potential principals go through several rounds of interviews with senior management, including the permanent secretary, director-general, and directors in the MOE. They also need to undergo the Leadership Situation Exercise, a 2-day intensive simulation test to gauge their leadership competencies and their readiness to take on leadership positions. After this selection process, they are required to attend the 6-month Leaders in Education Program (LEP) conducted by the NIE.

> Teachers with leadership potential are identified early and groomed for leadership.

The LEP is a leadership executive program that exposes potential school leaders to challenging leadership experiences in the context of the school and beyond to the other industries. Participants have the opportunity to visit other countries and learn about their educational systems and structures as well as the kinds of issues they are grappling with. The LEP also helps shape the personal qualities for effective leadership and prepare them to meet the demands of school management and interactions with parents, the school board, and the public. Participants of the LEP partner with and are mentored by experienced principals while they take courses at the NIE. Beyond the LEP, new principals are given inservice training on governance, human resource management, financial management, and management of media.

The placement of principals in schools is decided at the headquarters level, where they are matched to schools according to their leadership strengths and the profile and needs of the school. Teachers and parents do not have a role in the selection and placement of principals.

Like teachers, principals are evaluated using the EPMS. They are assessed on their performance and leadership competencies. The evaluation takes into consideration processes and results in the following areas: vision for the school, strategic planning and administration, development and management of staff, and management of resources and school processes. They are also assessed on their overall school performance, which includes student academic achievement as well as achievements in nonacademic domains such as arts and aesthetics, physical fitness and sports, social and emotional well-being, and student morale and leadership. These evaluations are used to determine their promotion and progression along the leadership track. Principals who are not performing will be counseled, coached, and, if need be, redeployed.

Principals who show strong leadership abilities and a broad vision for educational improvement are continually evaluated for promotion to the level of cluster superintendent and even a directorship within the MOE.

LESSONS LEARNED

Singapore aims to build a coherent system grounded in a common vision of teaching and learning—one that takes into account the diverse needs of students and helps them become creative thinkers and problem solvers in an increasingly technological world. This system has several key characteristics:

- Deep respect for the profession from the top levels of government and throughout the society
- Strong, common training for all teachers and leaders around these shared goals

- Systematic mentoring and induction for new teachers by trained senior teachers
- Continual development of educational knowledge, skills, and talent through extensive, governmentally subsidized professional development opportunities and a career ladder offering roles that expand and share expertise
- Significant scheduled time for teachers to collaborate and learning together through lesson study, action research, and other reflections on practice

The Ministry of Education and the National Institute of Education take it as their responsibility to manage all of these features of the profession so that all teachers receive wide-ranging supports and the quality of teaching is strong across the system as a whole.

CHAPTER 6

Lessons from Successful Systems

Linda Darling-Hammond
Robert Rothman

There are some lessons that can be learned from a look at both the U.S. experience and that of more successful systems. The stories of Finland, Ontario, and Singapore, as well as the earlier experiments in Connecticut and North Carolina, illustrate that the right efforts to improve teacher effectiveness can lead to higher and more equitable student achievement. The requisite elements appear to include:

- A systemic approach
- Strong recruitment and preparation
- Attractive teaching conditions
- Continual support for learning
- Equitable allocation of teachers and resources
- Proactive leadership development

From these components and the ways in which they support the successes of high-performing systems, we can draw six important lessons that can be applied to our own.

LESSON 1: IT TAKES A SYSTEM

While the educator-development systems of Finland, Ontario, and Singapore differ in significant ways, what they have in common is that they are just that—*systems* for teacher and leader development. They include multiple components, not just a single policy, and these components are intended to be coherent and complementary, to support the overall goal of ensuring that each school in each jurisdiction is filled with highly effective teachers and is led by a highly effective principal (see Figure 6.1). The more short-lived experiences of Connecticut and North Carolina illustrate the same point, and produced similar results in terms of educator effectiveness and higher student performance.

This vision of a system of educator development is sometimes described in terms of "human capital management," as a people-centered approach is termed in business. This framework draws organizational attention to recruiting, developing, and retaining talented individuals, and to focusing leaders on supporting their effectiveness. In creating a human capital system, organizations might start with a component that addresses their most urgent need, but they recognize that all of the elements require attention and need to work together effectively.

The systems we have highlighted here encompass the full range of policies that affect the development and support for teachers and school leaders, including the recruitment of qualified individuals into the profession, their preparation, their induction, their professional development, their evaluation and career development, and their retention over time. Leaders in these jurisdictions recognize that all of these policies need to work in harmony or the system will become unbalanced.

> This framework draws organizational attention to recruiting, developing, and retaining talented individuals.

For example, placing too strong an emphasis on recruitment without concomitant attention on development and retention could result in a continual churn within the teaching profession.

That said, each of the jurisdictions has chosen to place its primary focus on particular aspects of the system. Finland, for example, has sought since 1979 to invest intensely in the initial preparation of teachers. That year, the country required all teachers, including those teaching in the primary grades, to earn at least a master's degree in education, in addition to a bachelor's degree in one or more content areas. To complement the powerful initial preparation, Finland then provides teachers with considerable support—primarily, time to collaborate with their peers to develop curricula and assessments—and considerable autonomy.

> All of these policies need to work in harmony or the system will become unbalanced.

Ontario, meanwhile, emphasizes building the capacity of the teaching workforce. The province has instituted a comprehensive induction program for new teachers that includes professional development and appraisal, as well

Figure 6.1. An Educator Development System

as an appraisal program for all teachers that focuses on development and growth. These policies are intended to complement the strong initial preparation that all teachers receive and have served to reverse an exodus from the teaching profession.

Singapore augments its strong initial preparation and induction with a highly developed performance management system, which spells out the knowledge, skills, and attitudes expected at each stage of a teacher's career and, based on careful evaluation and intensive supports, provides a series of career tracks that teachers can pursue. These enable teachers to become mentor teachers, curriculum specialists, or principals, thereby developing talent in every component of the education system.

The systems in all three jurisdictions are continually being refined. Finland's Ministry of Education has become concerned that teachers need more support, so the country is considering strengthening induction and professional development for practicing teachers. Ontario surveyed teachers and found that there were some gaps in initial preparation, in areas like classroom management and teaching students with special needs, so the province recently overhauled the expectations for teacher education and revamped its induction system to address those areas. Singapore is looking to strengthen instruction in skills such as problem solving and critical thinking that are increasingly important in a global economy and society.

LESSON 2: GET IT RIGHT FROM THE START

Leaders in Finland, Ontario, and Singapore all believe that getting the right people into teaching and preparing them well is a critical piece in teacher development. All of these systems have strong systems for recruiting and preparing teachers.

Recruitment and Selection

In each jurisdiction, entry into teacher education programs is extremely selective. Finland chooses 1 out of every 10 individuals who apply to become primary school teachers; Singapore has traditionally chosen participants into undergraduate programs from the top third of high school grades (the nation is now moving rapidly toward graduate-level preparation); and in Ontario, where graduate-level preparation is also the norm, the process is highly competitive. In that way, each jurisdiction helps ensure that highly capable people go into teaching. Some states in the United States meet this kind of standard.

Finland, Ontario, and Singapore not only recruit able candidates, but they also screen them carefully to ensure that they have the attributes that make teachers effective—including commitment to the profession and evidence of the capacity to work well with children, as well as academic ability. In Finland, for example, a two-stage process looks first for top academic honors and then examines students' understanding of teaching—both through a written exam on pedagogy and their participation in a clinical activity that replicates a school situation and demonstrates social interaction and communication skills as well as teaching attitudes and behaviors. Finnish applicants to teacher preparation also complete exercises that evaluate whether they can read and understand research articles, and interpret their findings, since the master's degree program emphasizes teachers' abilities to use and conduct practical research to inform their practice.

As we note below, recruitment is aided by the fact that teaching pays good wages and teacher preparation is subsidized, so that candidates do not have to go into debt to prepare themselves for a field in which they will earn less than they would in other professional fields. All of these things, plus the positive cultural messages that are communicated about teachers and teaching, make education a desirable occupational choice.

Preparation

Once selected, applicants for teaching in each jurisdiction go through carefully designed and well-supported preparation programs. In Finland, teachers must earn at least a 2-year master's degree in education at one of eight universities that are known internationally for their rigorous, research-based programs. This degree follows on undergraduate training in a major subject plus two minor subjects. Teachers both study research and become researchers: They complete a master's thesis on a pedagogical problem.

A substantial amount of the time spent in teacher education is in clinical practice in one of the model schools that partner with each university. In these schools, teachers are specially selected and trained to be sure they can model effective practice and coach beginners. University courses also model strategies of cooperative and problem-based learning, reflective practice, and computer-supported education, encouraged by a higher education evaluation system that rewards effective, innovative university teaching practice.

Ontario teachers also go through rigorous preparation at one of 13 universities accredited by the Ontario College of Teachers. These programs generally consist of 3 or 4 years of undergraduate study, plus 2 years of teacher preparation at a faculty of education, where teachers earn a degree specializing in teacher education and engage in at least 80 days of clinical learning in school-based practicum experiences. Like Finland's model schools, a growing number of universities are following the lead of the University of Toronto, which engages professional development school partners in supporting student teaching in a context of ongoing teacher development and school renewal.

Singapore revamped its teacher education programs in 2001 to increase teachers' pedagogical knowledge and skills as well as content knowledge. Singapore has been moving toward graduate-level training of teachers, with about two-thirds now completing a 1-year master's degree program following the undergraduate content major, and one-third completing a 4-year undergraduate program. All teachers, including those who will teach in elementary schools, must demonstrate deep mastery of at least one content area (plus study of other subjects they will teach), and clinical training has been expanded. A new school partnership model engages schools more proactively in supporting trainees during their practicum experiences.

All preservice preparation occurs in the National Institute of Education, affiliated with Nanyang Technological University. At NIE, candidates learn to teach in the same way they will be asked to teach. Every student has a laptop, and the entire campus is wireless. The library spaces and a growing number of classrooms are consciously arranged with round tables and groups of three to four chairs so that students will have places to share knowledge and collaborate. Comfortable areas with sofa and chair arrangements are designed for group-work among teachers and principals, with access to full technology supports (e.g., video recording and computer hookup, and a plasma screen for projecting their work as they do it). During the course of preparation, there is a focus on teaching for problem-based and inquiry learning, on developing collaboration, and on addressing a range of learning styles in the classroom.

Significantly, all three jurisdictions subsidize the preparation of teachers. In Finland and Singapore, teacher education is paid for completely by the government, and candidates earn a stipend or a salary while they train. In Ontario, the government provides faculties of education with funding to cover a quota of student places, which subsidizes most of the costs of preparation; the remainder is covered by student fees. With those subsidies, promising students can enter teacher education knowing that they will not carry large debts once they graduate.

While there are some equally successful schools of education in the United States that have actually helped to inform the models in these countries (see Darling-Hammond, 2006; Levine, 2006), there is no state that has adopted a common model of preparation or that fully subsidizes the preparation of all teachers. The subsidies for supporting teacher training have dwindled considerably since the 1960s and 1970s, when there were large federal commitments. States have sometimes created subsidies for teachers in shortage areas, but these have not been sufficiently sizable or consistent to fully address the problems. Now policy incentives frequently make more funds available for alternative routes that cut corners than for high-quality programs that produce stronger outcomes. Consequently, teachers often get only as much preparation as they happen into or feel they can afford, rather than as much as they may want and need.

> All three jurisdictions subsidize the preparation of teachers.

> Equally successful schools of education in the United States have actually helped to inform the models in these countries.

Induction

In Ontario and Singapore, when new teachers enter the profession, they also experience an extensive set of formal induction supports. (In Finland, mentoring is organized at the school level.) In Singapore, beginning teachers receive 2 years of coaching from expert senior teachers who are trained by the National Institute of Education as mentors and are given released time to help beginners learn their craft. During the structured mentoring period, beginning teachers teach a reduced load (about two-thirds that of an experienced teacher) and attend courses in classroom management, counseling, reflective practices, and assessment offered by the National Institute of Education and the Ministry of Education.

In Ontario, the New Teacher Induction Program provides a range of supports, including orientation, mentoring, and professional development focused on key areas of need identified by new teachers, including classroom management, communication with parents, assessment and evaluation, and work with special-needs students. This 2-year program of supports—which school boards are required to offer and new teachers are required to participate in—has greatly reduced the attrition of beginning teachers across the state.

Along with collaborative planning time and a reduced teaching load, these are the features of high-quality induction programs found in U.S. studies to be associated with strong outcomes, including high teacher retention rates (Ingersoll, 2012). There are states in the United States that have developed high-quality induction programs that aim to make many of these supports widely available (initially California, Connecticut, and North Carolina, and most notably in recent years, Iowa and South Carolina); however, resources for such programs have been significantly affected by budget cuts, and relatively few offer state-funded mentoring today. Although estimates suggest that at least 80% of beginning teachers in the United States have access to some form of induction, only about 5% have access to the combination of supports that are routine for novices in Ontario and Singapore (Ingersoll, 2012).

> Although estimates suggest that at least 80% of beginning teachers in the United States have access to some form of induction, only about 5% have access to the combination of supports that are routine for novices in Ontario and Singapore.

LESSON 3: MAKE TEACHING AN ATTRACTIVE PROFESSION

Finland, Ontario, and Singapore have been able to attract and retain highly effective teachers in part because, in each jurisdiction, teaching is an attractive profession, one that many individuals want to join and stay in. In Finland, for example, college students who are surveyed rank teaching as a top-rated job. Unlike the United States, where talented college graduates who choose to enter education are often asked, "Why would you want to teach?" teaching is a draw for academically talented youth, who are eager to enter and stay in the profession.

In some respects, this attractiveness is a cultural phenomenon. Leaders have frequently expressed their belief that teachers are vital, and that has helped raise the status of the profession. In 1966, when Singapore had just achieved its independence, then-Minister of Education Ong Pang Boon declared that "the future of every one of us in Singapore is to a large extent determined by what our teachers do in the classroom." Forty years later, Singapore's prime minister, Lee Hsien Loong, reaffirmed this commitment: "Just as a country is as good as its people, so its citizens are only as good as their teachers."

The respect accorded to teachers is not all about money. While new teachers in Singapore are paid nearly as well as new doctors entering government service, Finland's teachers—among the most admired professionals in the country—earn about the average Finnish salary, the equivalent to the average of mid-career teachers in OECD nations, about 41,000 USD (OECD, 2010a). Salaries in Ontario, as in most of Canada, are competitive with those of other college graduates, and have contributed to substantial surpluses of teachers.

Beyond ensuring reasonable compensation, each jurisdiction has developed and implemented policies that make teaching attractive, and these efforts have clearly paid off. In addition to rhetorical support, leaders have adopted policies to improve teachers' working conditions and sense of professionalism, elevating teaching to the level of other professions like medicine and law.

> Beyond ensuring reasonable compensation, each jurisdiction has adopted policies to improve teachers' working conditions and sense of professionalism.

Finland has built professionalism into its system. Because teachers are so well prepared, they are also well respected and much trusted, receiving high status in the society and operating with significant autonomy inside the classroom. Teachers' work is compared to that of medical doctors. The country has no external tests, except for samples taken at two grade levels and a faculty-developed admissions test for college. Instead, the nation relies on teachers to develop their own assessments of student learning based on the National Curriculum. In that way, the country has signaled that teachers are professionals who can make sound judgments about student progress. There is no formal evaluation process, but teachers receive continual feedback from their principal and from other school faculty members.

Furthermore, teaching conditions in Finland are highly desirable. Schools are equitably funded, well stocked, and uniformly well supported; class sizes are fairly small; students receive food and health care as well as educational supports. In addition, teachers' instructional hours are short by U.S. standards (about 60% of the time U.S. teachers teach); thus teachers have time for fashioning strong instruction, planning, meeting with students and parents, and grading papers, while maintaining a reasonable family life. Only 10% to 15% of teachers leave the profession during the course of their career, an attrition rate of less than 1% per year.

In Ontario, teachers are supported in using research to improve their practice and their schools, and they are recognized when their efforts succeed. Teachers can also earn more as they gain expertise by completing Additional Qualifications programs that enhance their knowledge and skills in such areas as special education, English as a second language, and French as a second language.

As part of its efforts to professionalize teaching, Ontario ended several policies adopted in the 1990s, such as testing and evaluation requirements that teachers had seen as punitive, which had led to an exodus from the profession. The incoming Liberal government, which took office in 2003, instead created a Working Table on Teacher Development that included teacher representatives and adopted policies aimed at providing support and building teachers' capacity to teach more effectively. The province now has a surplus of teachers, as do Finland and Singapore.

Few teachers leave the profession in any of these jurisdictions. In Singapore, the attrition rate of teachers is less than 3% annually, which is one-third of the annual attrition rate for teachers in the United States. Based on a recent Ministry of Education survey, teachers rank the following three reasons as key to staying in teaching: positive culture with a strong sense of mission; good compensation and rewards benchmarked against market rates; and a wide range of opportunities for professional growth and development.

Singapore's performance-management system and career-ladder program help to create a strong profession. Teachers have numerous opportunities to grow professionally and take on leadership responsibilities, based on demonstrations of competence. Depending on their own abilities and career goals, teachers can remain in the classroom and become lead and master teachers; they can take on specialist roles, like curriculum

Few teachers leave the profession in any of these jurisdictions.

specialist or guidance counselor; or they can take the leadership track and become administrators. The Ministry of Education is constantly looking for ways to recognize and promote teacher leadership, both for individuals who have demonstrated various talents and for teachers as a whole.

In the United States, aside from the Teachers of the Year competition and some foundation-funded awards, there are few governmental supports or recognitions for teachers that match those that are found in other countries. Career-ladder programs have come and gone in several waves of reform. With budget cuts, incentives for National Board Certification have been lost in a number of states and districts, and in many states the political discourse around getting rid of bad teachers has replaced the discussion about recruiting and retaining good ones.

LESSON 4: INVEST IN CONTINUAL LEARNING

In addition to providing strong initial preparation for teachers and creating working conditions that encourage retention, each of these jurisdictions also provides opportunities and support for teachers to develop their knowledge and skills, to improve their practice, and to grow as professionals. All three jurisdictions provide considerable time for teachers to work collaboratively and learn together during the regular school schedule —as much as five times what U.S. teachers receive. This enables teachers to become both individually and collectively more effective and helps ensure that highly effective teachers remain in schools.

Such efforts are critically important to avoid the disruption and cost associated with teacher attrition. In the United States, about one-third of beginning teachers leave the profession within 5 years, costing districts $7.3 billion a year (NCTAF, 2007). Teachers are most likely to leave if they feel ineffective or unsupported.

Singaporean teachers have about 20 hours a week built into their schedule for shared planning and learning, including visits to one another's classrooms, as well as 100 hours per year of state-supported professional development outside of their school time. The NIE and MOE have trained teachers for lesson study and action research in the classroom so that they can examine teaching and learning problems, and find solutions that can be disseminated to others. The MOE established a Teachers' Academy to support teacher-initiated and teacher-led learning opportunities around subject matter across schools. This incorporates the activities of the previously named Teachers Network, including learning circles, teacher-led workshops, conferences, and a website and publications series for sharing knowledge. The Academy has added additional initiatives to create subject-based Professional Learning Communities within and across schools. To support school-based learning, senior and master teachers are appointed to lead the coaching and development of the teachers in each school.

Singapore's performance-management system is designed explicitly to link to professional development and to provide growth opportunities for effective teachers. The system's career paths for teachers allow them to remain in the classroom and become lead or master teachers; to take on additional responsibilities, such as curriculum development, part-time or full-time, within the school or all the way up to the Ministry of Education; or to follow the leadership track and become school, district, regional, or national leaders in the education system.

All teacher and leadership training in Singapore is at government expense. As teachers are promoted and selected into these kinds of roles, they receive free courses of study through the MOE at the National Institute of Education, sometimes while they are still teaching and other times while taking a sabbatical from their jobs. How far teachers advance depends on their interests and the competencies they demonstrate through the evaluation system. Greater compensation accompanies greater responsibility, and a teacher at the top of the master teacher track can earn as much as a school principal.

In Finland, opportunities for teachers to develop their practice are embedded within their daily work. Within the parameters of the National Curriculum, teachers engage in joint curriculum planning and approve the school-level curriculum. The importance of curriculum design in teacher practice has helped shift the focus of professional development from fragmented inservice training toward more systemic, theoretically grounded schoolwide improvement efforts.

Because Finnish teachers take on significant responsibility for curriculum and assessment, as well as experimentation with and improvement of teaching methods, some of the most important aspects of their work are conducted beyond traditional teaching roles. Teachers take on many of the roles conducted by educational consultants and specialists in other countries, but because teaching is highly professionalized, diverse responsibilities are handled within the teaching role, without teachers leaving teaching or being placed in more bureaucratically respected, highly compensated roles. Although the career structure is not hierarchical, experienced teachers earn much more than their peers in the United States.

Many Finnish teachers take advantage of the opportunity to pursue doctoral studies in education, often while simultaneously teaching school. According to a recent national survey, teachers devote about 7 working days per year on average to professional development on their own time and that provided by the system. The state plans to double its 30 million USD annual budget for professional development of teachers and school principals by 2016.

The Ontario Ministry of Education has adopted a multifaceted set of capacity-building strategies to support effective leadership, teaching, and student learning. Teachers and principals have 6 professional activity days every school year to work with one another on activities related to key state and local priorities. The ministry also fosters capacity building and collaboration by sharing information about existing and emerging successful practices in schools and classrooms through studies, webcasts, and videos of effective practices that can be used in professional development initiatives.

Ontario's annual evaluation system for teachers is also designed for professional growth. As part of the system, teachers complete an Annual Learning Plan that outlines growth goals for the year. This plan allows teachers and principals to work together to plan improvement strategies and identify needed professional development.

In addition, Ontario's Ministry of Education funds a Teacher Learning and Leadership Program, which provides job-embedded professional development for qualifying teachers. The program awards funding for teacher-led projects; participants join a province-wide network that shares ideas and best practices. This has motivated substantial innovation across the province. There are also opportunities for teachers and principals to work in the ministry on provincial policy and program development and assist with capacity building and implementation in partnership with the education system. This practice not only enhances teachers' knowledge and skills, but it also improves ministry policies and strategies by giving teachers a hand in setting them and ensuring that they can be implemented effectively.

LESSON 5: PUTTING SUFFICIENT RESOURCES WHERE THEY ARE MOST NEEDED

A feature of all successful systems is the recognition that the quality of any child's education should not depend on the income of his or her family. Differences in family resources exist in all societies, perhaps nowhere more than in the United States, where the income gap between rich and poor has stretched to its widest in recent years. High-performing systems in Singapore, Finland, and Ontario ensure that family income differences do not put a ceiling on student learning.

All three fund schools equitably; in addition, they recruit and prepare all teachers well and create incentives to ensure they are equitably distributed among the schools. These include uniform salary schedules that ensure adequate compensation across each jurisdiction and mentoring supports so that teachers do not struggle in schools where students have greater needs.

Similarly, in Connecticut and North Carolina, reforms equalized student access to high-quality teachers by simultaneously increasing the quality of preparation and induction while raising and equalizing salaries, so that all districts could compete in the labor market for well-qualified teachers.

In these states, as in the three countries we highlight here, a more equitable funding base was joined with stronger training to reduce reliance on underprepared or emergency-certified teachers. The more teachers understand about how to be teach effectively, the less likely they are to leave the field, which also decreases churn in higher-need schools.

> In Connecticut and North Carolina, reforms equalized student access to high-quality teachers.

LESSON 6: PROACTIVELY RECRUIT AND DEVELOP HIGH-QUALITY LEADERSHIP

One of the most significant aspects of the educator-development systems in Finland, Ontario, and Singapore is their investment in leadership development and support. These systems recognize that high-quality leadership strengthens teaching by providing skillful guidance and creating a school vision that teachers share.

The evidence shows that school leadership is second only to teaching in its effects on student learning. About a fourth of the school-related variation in student achievement can be explained by school leadership (Leithwood, Louis, Anderson, & Wahlstrom, 2004).

In all three jurisdictions, school leaders are expected to be *instructional leaders*. They are expected to know curriculum and teaching intimately and be able to provide guidance and support to teachers. While management and budgeting are important aspects of leaders' jobs, their instructional leadership role is paramount. Effective instructional leaders can evaluate teachers skillfully, provide them with useful feedback, assess the school's needs for professional development, and direct instructional resources where they are most needed. Principals are attuned to the learning needs of students and adults.

> School leadership is second only to teaching in its effects on student learning.

To help ensure that all leaders can fulfill this role, all three jurisdictions proactively recruit principals from among the ranks of expert teachers who exhibit leadership potential. In Finland, principals by law must be qualified to teach in the school they lead. That means not only that someone from outside of education cannot become a principal, but also that an elementary teacher cannot become a principal in a high school.

The three jurisdictions also provide principal training that is designed to ensure they can assume the instructional leadership role expected of them. In Ontario, prospective principals take part in a Principals' Qualifications Program accredited by the Ontario College of Teachers, which consists of two parts, each totalling 125 hours, plus a practicum. The program, which is structured around the Ontario Leadership Framework, emphasizes instructional leadership. Support is provided by faculties of education and principals' associations. In addition to completing the PQP, principals must have an undergraduate degree, 5 years of classroom experience, qualifications in three divisions of the school system, and a master's degree or other equivalent studies. Once appointed, all principals and vice principals receive mentoring for their first 2 years in each role. This mentoring, fully funded by the ministry, is organized around a learning plan to guide the support.

In Singapore, teachers with leadership potential are identified early and groomed for leadership positions, generally progressing to subject head, head of department, vice principal, and then principal. Potential principals, who are selected after a grueling interview process that includes a 2-day simulation test, enter the 6-month Leaders in Education program. This program, conducted by the Ministry of Education, includes education coursework, field-based projects, and mentoring from senior principals, as well as examinations of other industries and visits to other countries to learn about effective practices.

All of the leadership programs also include extensive clinical training. In Finland, for example, some university-based programs include a peer-assisted leadership model, in which part of the training is done by shadowing and being mentored by the senior school principal.

> All of the leadership programs include extensive clinical training.

CONCLUSION

Taken individually, these lessons might sound familiar to American ears. Many districts and states have programs in place that reflect at least some of them. They have instituted programs to recruit highly capable individuals into teaching and prepare them effectively, provided ongoing support and development along with career paths for veteran teachers, and have invested in high-quality leadership.

These efforts, however, as promising as they are, do not yet add up to a *system* in most communities. While some states may be viewing teacher development systemically, most are not, and many of the initiatives are tackling the issue in a piecemeal fashion. And few states or districts have created a seamless, well-supported pipeline to school leadership positions. As the examples from high-performing nations show, only a systemic approach will ensure that all schools and classrooms are staffed by highly effective leaders and teachers.

Each high-performing system began with the recognition that its system needed improvement. Each experienced significant challenges and determined a primary focus for its initial efforts. In Finland, it was teacher candidate screening, recruitment, and preparation. In Ontario, it was deep and focused professional development for teachers and principals. In Singapore, it was creating a strong system of teacher supports that eventually developed into a career system providing extensive training and peer supports. In each case, the starting point was a means for ultimately developing a coherent system of learning and support for teaching. As success was achieved in one area, new goals were set to ensure that success

> Each high-performing system began with the recognition that its system needed improvement.

was supported and expanded into all of the areas influencing who enters teaching, and how they are prepared, developed, evaluated, compensated, and supported in their work.

> As success was achieved in one area, new goals were set.

States in the United States can begin, as these systems have, by tackling the highest-leverage concerns in their own context. North Carolina and Connecticut have shown that strategic and comprehensive investments in teaching are possible and can succeed. Our challenge is to sustain these kinds of productive policies, understanding that our future depends on the education of our children, and their education depends on the success of our teachers.

References

Adamson, F., & Darling-Hammond, L. (2012). Funding disparities and the inequitable distribution of teachers: Evaluating sources and solutions. *Education Policy Analysis Archives, 20*(37). Retrieved from epaa.asu.edu/ojs/article/view/1053

Aho, E., Pitkänen, K., & Sahlberg, P. (2006). *Policy development and reform principles of basic and secondary education in Finland since 1968.* Washington, DC: World Bank.

Auguste, B., Kihn, P., & Miller, M. (2010). *Closing the talent gap: Attracting and retaining top-third graduates to careers in teaching.* New York, NY: McKinsey.

Berry, B., Montgomery, D., Curtis, R. E., Hernandez, M., Wurtzel, J., & Snyder, J. D. (2010). Creating and sustaining urban teacher residencies. In R. E. Curtis & J. Wurtzel (Eds.), *Teaching talent: A visionary framework for human capital in education* (pp. 129–150). Cambridge, MA: Harvard Education Press.

Betts, J. R., Rueben, K. S., & Danenberg, A. (2000). *Equal resources, equal outcomes? The distribution of school resources and student achievement in California.* San Francisco, CA: Public Policy Institute of California.

Boyd, D., Grossman, P., Lankford, H., Loeb, S., & Wyckoff, J. (2006). How changes in entry requirements alter the teacher workforce and affect student achievement. *Education Finance & Policy, 1*(2), 176–216.

Boyd, D., Grossman, P., Lankford, H., Loeb, S., & Wyckoff, J. (2008, September). *Teacher preparation and student achievement* (NBER Working Paper No. w14314). Cambridge, MA: National Bureau of Economic Research. Retrieved from ssrn.com/abstract=1264576

Briggs, D. & Domingue, B. (2011). *Due diligence and the evaluation of teachers: A review of the value-added analysis underlying the effectiveness rankings of Los Angeles unified school district teachers by the Los Angeles Times.* Boulder, CO: National Education Policy Center.

Campbell, C., Lieberman, A., & Yashkina, A. (2013a). Teacher learning and leadership for classroom, school and system improvement. *Pensamiento Educativo: Revista de Investigación Educacional Latino Americana, 50*(2), 51–68. Retrieved from pensamientoeducativo.uc.cl/index.php/pel/article/view/594/1218

Campbell, C., Lieberman, A., & Yashkina, A. (2013b). *The teacher learning and leadership program: Research project.* Toronto, Canada: Ontario Teachers'

Federation. Retrieved from www.otffeo.on.ca/en/wp-content/uploads/sites/2/2013/09/tllp_full_report-.pdf (Executive Summary available at www.otffeo.on.ca/en/wp-content/uploads/sites/2/2013/09/tllp_summary.pdf)

Carnegie Task Force on Teaching as a Profession. (1986). *A nation prepared: Teachers for the 21st century.* Washington, DC: Carnegie Forum on Education and the Economy.

Carroll, T. G., & Foster, E. (2010). *Who will teach? Experience matters.* Washington, DC: National Commission on Teaching and America's Future.

Chetty, R., Friedman, J. N., & Rockoff, J. E. (2011, December). *The long-term impact of teachers: Teacher value-added and student outcomes in adulthood* (NBER Working Paper 17699). Cambridge, MA: National Bureau of Economic Research.

Choy, S. P., Chen, X., & Bugarin, R. (2006). *Teacher professional development in 1999–2000: What teachers, principals, and district staff report* (NCES 2006-305). Washington, DC: U.S. Department of Education, Institute of Education Sciences, National Center for Education Statistics.

Chuan, G. K., & Gopinathan, S. (2005). *Recent changes in primary teacher education in Singapore: Beyond design and implementation.* Singapore: National Institute of Education.

Clotfelter, C., Ladd, H., & Vigdor, J. (2007). *How and why do teacher credentials matter for student achievement?* (NBER Working Paper No. 12828). Cambridge, MA: National Bureau of Economic Research.

Curriculum Services Canada & Ontario Ministry of Education. (2013). *Webcasts for educators.* Retrieved from www.curriculum.org/k-12/en/

Darling-Hammond, L. (2006). *Powerful teacher education.* San Francisco, CA: Jossey-Bass.

Darling-Hammond, L. (2010). *The flat world and education: How America's commitment to equity will determine our future.* New York, NY: Teachers College Press.

Darling-Hammond, L. (2013). *Getting teacher evaluation right: What really matters for effectiveness and improvement.* New York, NY: Teachers College Press.

Darling-Hammond, L., Amrein-Beardsley, A., Haertel, E., & Rothstein, J. (2012). Evaluating teacher evaluation. *Phi Delta Kappan, 93*(6), 8–15.

Darling-Hammond, L., & Falk, B. (2014). Supporting teacher learning through performance assessment. In L. Darling-Hammond & F. Adamson (Eds)., *Beyond the bubble test: How performance assessments support 21st century learning* (pp. 207–236). San Francisco, CA: Jossey-Bass.

Darling-Hammond, L., Holtzman, D., Gatlin, S. J., & Heilig, J. V. (2005). Does teacher preparation matter? Evidence about teacher certification, Teach for America, and teacher effectiveness. *Education Policy Analysis Archives, 13*(42). Retrieved from epaa.asu.edu/ojs/article/view/147

Darling-Hammond, L., Newton, S. P., & Wei, R. C. (2013). Developing and assessing beginning teacher effectiveness: The potential of performance assessments. *Educational Assessment, Evaluation and Accountability, 25*(3), 179–204. Retrieved from link.springer.com/article/10.1007/s11092-013-9163-0

Darling-Hammond, L., & Sykes, G. (Eds.). (1999). *Teaching as the learning profession: Handbook of policy and practice.* San Francisco, CA: Jossey-Bass.

Darling-Hammond, L., Wei, R. C., Andree, A., Richardson, N., & Orphanos, S. (2009). *Professional learning in the learning profession: A status report on teacher development in the United States and abroad.* Washington, DC: National Staff Development Council.

Davis, S., Darling-Hammond, L., LaPointe, M., & Meyerson, D. (2005). *Developing successful principals.* Stanford, CA: Stanford Educational Leadership Institute.

Decker, P. T., Mayer, D. P., & Glazerman, S. (2004). *The effects of Teach for America on students: Findings from a national evaluation.* Princeton, NJ: Mathematica.

Dixon, Q. L. (2005). Bilingual education policy in Singapore: An analysis of its sociohistorical roots and current academic outcomes. *International Journal of Bilingual Education and Bilingualism, 8*(1), 25–47.

edTPA. (n.d.). Participation map. Retrieved from edtpa.aacte.org/state-policy

Finnish National Board of Education. (n.d.). *Teachers in Finland—trusted professionals.* Helsinki, Finland: Author. Retrieved from http://www.oph.fi/download/148960_Teachers_in_Finland.pdf

Fullan, M., Hill, P., & Crevola, C. (2006). *Breakthrough.* Thousand Oaks, CA: Corwin Press.

Gitomer, D. H. (2008). *Teacher quality in a changing policy landscape: Improvements in the teaching pool.* Princeton, NJ: Educational Testing Service.

Glazerman, S., & Seifullah, A. (2012). *An evaluation of the Chicago Teacher Advancement Program (Chicago TAP) after four years: Final report.* New York, NY: Mathematica.

Goh, C. B., & Gopinathan, S. (2008). The development of education in Singapore since 1965. In S.-K. Lee, C. B. Goh, B. Fredriksen, & J.-P. Tan (Eds.), *Toward a better future: Education and training for economic development in Singapore since 1965* (pp. 12–38). Washington, DC: World Bank.

Goldhaber, D. D., & Brewer, D. J. (1998, October). When should we reward degrees for teachers? *Phi Delta Kappan, 80*(2), 134–138.

Goldhaber, D. D., Brewer, D. J., & Anderson, D. (1999). A three-way error components analysis of educational productivity. *Education Economics, 7*(3), 199–208.

Hallinger, P. (1992) School leadership development: evaluating a decade of reform, *Education and Urban Society, 24*(3), 300–316.

Hargreaves, A., Halasz, G., & Pont, B. (2008). The Finnish approach to system leadership. In B. Pont, D. Nusche, & D. Hopkins (Eds.), *Improving school leadership: Vol. 2. Case studies on system leadership* (pp. 69–109). Paris, France: OECD.

Haynes, D. D. (1995). One teacher's experience with National Board assessment. *Educational Leadership*, 52, 58–60.

Haynes, M. (2011, February). *Transforming high schools: Performance systems for powerful teaching*. Washington, DC: Alliance for Excellent Education.

Henry, G. T., Bastian, K. C., & Smith, A. A. (2012). *The North Carolina Teaching fellows program: A comprehensive evaluation*. Chapel Hill, NC: Education Policy Initiative at Carolina.

Holmes Group. (1986). *Tomorrow's teachers*. East Lansing, MI: Holmes Group.

Holmes Group. (1990). *Tomorrow's schools*. East Lansing, MI: Holmes Group.

Ingersoll, R. (2012). Beginning teacher induction: What the data tell us. *Phi Delta Kappan, 93*(8), 47–51.

Ingersoll, R., & Merrill, L. (2012, April). *The changing face of the teaching profession: Implications for policy*. Paper presented at the annual meeting of the American Educational Research Association, Vancouver, BC, Canada.

Jakku-Sihvonen, R., & Niemi, H. (Eds.). (2006). *Research-based teacher education in Finland: Reflections by Finnish teacher educators* (Research Report 25). Turku, Finland: Finnish Educational Research Association.

Jussila, J., & Saari, S. (Eds.). (2000). *Teacher education as a future-molding factor: International evaluation of teacher education in Finnish universities*. Helsinki: Higher Education Evaluation Council.

Kane, T. J., Rockoff, J. E., & Staiger, D. O. (2006). *What does certification tell us about teacher effectiveness? Evidence from New York City* (NBER Working Paper No. W12155). Cambridge, MA: National Bureau of Economic Research.

Kangasniemi, S. (2008). With which profession to get married? *Helsingin Sanomat Koulutusliite*, 4–6.

Lankford, H., Loeb, S., & Wyckoff, J. (2002). Teacher sorting and the plight of urban schools: A descriptive analysis. *Education Evaluation and Policy Analysis, 24*(1), 37–62.

Leithwood, K. (2012). *The Ontario Leadership Framework 2012: with a discussion of the research foundations*. Toronto, ON, Canada: Ontario Institute for Education Leadership. Retrieved from iel.immix.ca/storage/6/1360068388/Final_Research_Report_-_EN_REV_Feb_4_2013.pdf

Leithwood, K., Louis, K. S., Anderson, S., & Wahlstrom, K. (2004). *How leadership influences student learning*. Minneapolis, MN: University of Minnesota, Center for Applied Research and Educational Improvement; and Toronto, ON, Canada: University of Toronto, Ontario Institute for Studies in Education.

Levin, B. (2008). *How to change 5000 schools: A practical and positive approach for leading change at every level*. Cambridge, MA: Harvard Education Press.

Levine, A. (2006). *Educating school teachers*. Washington, DC: The Education Schools Project.

Liiten, M. (2004, February 11). Ykkössuosikki: Opettajan ammatti [Top favorite: Teaching profession]. *Helsingin Sanomat*. Retrieved from www.hs.fi/artikkeli/Ykk%C3%B6ssuosikki+opettajan+ammatti/1076151893860

Marsh, J. A., Springer, M. G., McCaffrey, D. F., Yuan, K., Epstein, S., Koppich, J., . . . Peng, A. (2011). *A big apple for educators: New York City's experiment with schoolwide performance bonuses: Final evaluation report.* Santa Monica, CA: Rand.

McCaffrey, D. F., Koretz, D. M., Lockwood, J. R., & Hamilton, L. S. (2004). *The promise and peril of using value-added modeling to measure teacher effectiveness* (Research Brief No. RB-9050-EDU). Santa Monica, CA: RAND Corporation.

Mehta, J. D., & Schwartz, R. B. (2011). Canada: looks a lot like us but gets much better results. In M. S. Tucker (Ed.), *Surpassing Shanghai: An agenda for American education built on the world's leading systems* (pp. 141–166). Cambridge, MA: Harvard Education Press.

MetLife, Inc. (2012, March). *The MetLife survey of the American teacher: Teachers, parents, and the economy.* New York, NY: MetLife Foundation.

Ministry of Education. (2007). *Opettajankoulutus 2020 [Teacher Education 2020]* (Committee Report 2007: 44). Helsinki, Finland: Ministry of Education.

Ministry of Education. (2009). *Ensuring professional competence and improving opportunities for continuing education in education* (Committee Report 2009: 16). Helsinki, Finland: Ministry of Education.

Murphy, J. (1990). Principal instructional leadership. In R. S. Lotto & P. W. Thurston (Eds.), *Advances in educational administration: Changing perspectives on the school* (Vol. 1, Pt. B, pp. 163–200). Greenwich, CT: JAI.

National Board of Education. (2014). Opettajat Suomessa [Teachers in Finland]. Koulutuksen seurantaraportit, 8. Helsinki, Finland: National Board of Education.

National Board for Professional Teaching Standards (NBPTS). (n.d.). *What teachers should know and be able to do.* Detroit, MI: NBPTS.

National Board for Professional Teaching Standards (NBPTS) (2001, Fall). *The impact of National Board Certification on teachers: A survey of National Board Certified Teachers and assessors.* Washington, DC: Author.

National Commission on Teaching and America's Future (NCTAF). (1996). *What matters most: Teaching for America's future.* New York, NY: Teachers College, Columbia University.

National Commission on Teaching and America's Future (NCTAF). (1997). *Doing What Matters Most: Investing in Quality Teaching.* New York, NY: National Commission on Teaching and America's Future, Teachers College, Columbia University.

National Commission on Teaching and America's Future (NCTAF). (2007). *The high cost of teacher turnover: Policy brief.* Washington, DC: Author.

National Institute of Education (NIE). (2010). *TE21: A teacher education model for the 21st century.* Singapore: National Institute of Education. Retrieved from www.nie.edu.sg/about-nie/teacher-education-21

Newton, X., Darling-Hammond, L., Haertel, E., & Thomas, E. (2010). Value-added modeling of teacher effectiveness: An exploration of stability across models and contexts. *Educational Policy Analysis Archives, 18*(23). Retrieved from epaa.asu.edu/ojs/article/view/810

Ng, P. T. (2008). Educational reform in Singapore: From quantity to quality. *Education Research on Policy and Practice, 7*, 5–15.

OECD. (2010a). *Education at a Glance 2010: OECD Indicators.* Paris, France: OECD. Retrieved from www.oecd-ilibrary.org/education/education-at-a-glance-2010_eag-2010-en

OECD. (2010b). *PISA 2009 results: What students know and can do: Student performance in reading, mathematics and science* (Vol. 1). OECD Publishing. Retrieved from dx.doi.org/10.1787/9789264091450-en

OECD. (2013). *Education at a Glance: 2013.* Paris, France: OECD. Retrieved from http://www.oecd-ilibrary.org/education/education-at-a-glance-2013_eag-2013-en

OECD. (2014a). *Education at a Glance 2014: OECD Indicators.* OECD Publishing. Retrieved from www.oecd-ilibrary.org/education/education-at-a-glance-2014_eag-2014-en

OECD. (2014b). *TALIS 2013 Results: An international perspective on teaching and learning.* OECD Publishing. Retrieved from dx.doi.org/10.1787/9789264196261-en

Ontario College of Teachers (OCT). (2012). *Transition to Teaching 2012: Teachers face tough entry-job hurdles in an increasingly crowded Ontario employment market.* Retrieved from www.oct.ca/-/media/PDF/Transition%20to%20Teaching%202012/T2T%20Main%20Report_EN_web_accessible0313.pdf

Ontario College of Teachers (OCT). (2014). Professional standards. Retrieved from www.oct.ca/public/professional-standards

Ontario Ministry of Education. (n.d.) Retrieved from www.edu.gov.on.ca/eng/teacher/develop.html

Ontario Ministry of Education (2005). *Leading education: New supports for principals and vice-principals in Ontario publicly funded schools.* (v. 2). Toronto: Author.

Ontario Ministry of Education (2013a). Quick facts, Ontario schools, 2012–13. Toronto, Canada: Author. Retrieved from http://www.edu.gov.on.ca/eng/general/elemsec/quickfacts/2012-13/quickFacts12_13.pdf

Ontario Ministry of Education. (2013b). *Principal/vice-principal performance appraisal: Technical requirements manual, 2013.* Toronto, Canada: Queen's Printer for Ontario. Retrieved from www.edu.gov.on.ca/eng/policyfunding/leadership/PPA_Manual.pdf

Ontario Ministry of Education. (2013c). *2013 School Effectiveness Framework: A support for school improvement and student success, K–12.* Toronto, Canada: Queen's Printer for Ontario. Retrieved from www.edu.gov.on.ca/eng/literacynumeracy/SEF2013.pdf

Ontario Ministry of Education. (2014). *Achieving excellence: A renewed vision for education in Ontario.* Toronto, Canada: Queen's Printer for Ontario. Retrieved from www.edu.gov.on.ca/eng/about/renewedVision.pdf

Pecheone, R. L., & Chung, R. R. (2006). Evidence in teacher education: The Performance Assessment for California Teachers (PACT). *Journal of Teacher Education 57*(1), 22–36.

Piesanen, E., Kiviniemi, U., & Valkonen, S. (2007). *Follow-up and evaluation of the teacher education development program: Continuing teacher education in 2005 and its follow-up 1998–2005 by fields and teaching subjects in different types of educational institutions.* Jyväskylä, Finland: University of Jyväskylä, Institute for Educational Research.

Public Agenda. (2003). *Stand by me: What teachers really think about unions, merit pay, and other professional matters.* New York, NY: Public Agenda.

Rivkin, S. G., Hanushek, E. A., & Kain, J. F. (2000). *Teachers, schools, and academic achievement* [revised] (Working Paper No. 6691). Cambridge, MA: National Bureau of Economic Research.

Roza M., & Miller, R. (2009). *Separation of degrees: State-by-state analysis of teachers' compensation for master's degrees.* Washington, DC: Center for American Progress.

Sahlberg, P. (2010). Educational change in Finland. In A. Hargreaves, A. Lieberman, M. Fullan, & D. Hopkins (Eds.), *Second international handbook of educational change* (pp. 1–28). New York, NY: Springer.

Sahlberg, P. (2015). *Finnish lessons 2.0: What can the world learn from educational change in Finland?* (2nd ed.). New York, NY: Teachers College Press

Schleicher, A. (Ed.). (2012). *Preparing teachers and developing school leaders for the 21st century: Lessons from around the world.* Paris, France: OECD Publishing. doi: 10.1787/9789264174559-en Retrieved from www.oecd-ilibrary.org/education/preparing-teachers-and-developing-school-leaders-for-the-21st-century_9789264174559-en

Singapore Ministry of Education. (2014). *About us: Our vision.* Retrieved from www.moe.gov.sg/about/

Snyder, J., & Ebmeier, H. (1992). Empirical linkages among principal behaviors and intermediate outcomes: Implications for principal evaluation. *Peabody Journal of Education, 68*(1), 75–107.

Socias, M., Chambers, J., Esra, P., & Shambaugh, L. (2007). *The distribution of teaching and learning resources in California's middle and high schools* (Issues & Answers Report, REL 2007–No. 023). Washington, DC: U.S. Department of Education, Institute of Education Sciences, National Center for Education Evaluation and Regional Assistance, Regional Educational Laboratory West.

Springer, M. G., Ballou, D., Hamilton, L., Le, V-N., Lockwood, J. R., McCaffrey, D. F., . . . Stecher, B. M. (2010). *Teacher pay for performance: Experimental evidence from the project on incentives in teaching.* Nashville, TN: National Center on Performance Incentives, Peabody College, Vanderbilt University.

Statistics Finland. (n.d.). Education. Retrieved from www.stat.fi/til/kou_en.html

Thomas B. Fordham Foundation (1999, April). *The teachers we need and how to get more of them.* Washington, DC: Author.

Toch, T., & Rothman, R. (2008, January). *Rush to judgment: Teacher evaluation in public education*. Washington, DC: Education Sector.

Tripp, D. (2004). Teachers' networks: A new approach to the professional development of teachers in Singapore. In C. Day & J. Sachsm (Eds.), *International handbook on the continuing professional development of teachers* (pp. 191–214). Maidenhead, UK: Open University Press.

Tucker, M. S. (2011). How the top performers got there: Analysis . . . and synthesis. In M. S. Tucker (Ed.), *Surpassing Shanghai: An agenda for American education built on the world's leading systems* (pp. 169–210). Cambridge, MA: Harvard Education Press.

U.S. Department of Education, National Center for Education Statistics (NCES). (2007). *Schools and Staffing Survey (SASS): Public school teacher questionnaire, 2007–08: Table H120*. Retrieved from nces.ed.gov/surveys/ctes/tables/h120.asp

Wei, R. C., Darling-Hammond, L., Andree, A., Richardson, N., & Orphanos, S. (2009). *Professional learning in the learning profession: A status report on teacher development in the United States and abroad*. Dallas, TX: National Staff Development Council.

Westbury, I., Hansen, S-E., Kansanen, P., & Björkvist, O. (2005). Teacher education for research-based practice in expanded roles: Finland's experience. *Scandinavian Journal of Educational Research, 49*(5), 475–485.

Wiley, E. W., Spindler, E. R., & Subert, A. N. (2010, April). *Denver ProComp: An outcomes evaluation of Denver's alternative teacher compensation system, 2010 Report*. Boulder, CO: University of Colorado at Boulder, School of Education.

Wilson, S. M., Floden, R. E., & Ferrini-Mundy, J. (2001). *Teacher preparation research: Current knowledge, gaps, and recommendations*. Paper prepared for the U.S. Department of Education. Seattle, WA: Center for the Study of Teaching and Policy.

Wise, A. E., Darling-Hammond, L., McLaughlin, M. W., & Bernstein, H. T. (1984). *Teacher evaluation: A study of effective practices*. Santa Monica, CA: Rand.

Xu, Z., Hannaway, J., & Taylor, C. (2009). *Making a difference? The effects of teach for America in high school*. Washington, DC: Urban Institute.

Yoon, K. S., Duncan, T., Lee, S., Scarloss, B., & Shapley, K. (2007). *Reviewing the evidence on how teacher professional development affects student achievement* (Issues & Answers Report, REL 2007–No. 033). Washington, DC: U.S. Department of Education, Institute of Education Sciences, National Center for Education Evaluation & Regional Assistance, Regional Educational Laboratory Southwest.

Index

About the Authors

Linda Darling-Hammond is Charles E. Ducommun Professor of Education at Stanford University, where she launched the Stanford Educational Leadership Institute, the Stanford Center on Opportunity Policy in Education (SCOPE), and the School Redesign Network. She has also served as faculty sponsor for the Stanford Teacher Education Program. She is former president of the American Educational Research Association and a member of the National Academy of Education. Her research, teaching, and policy work focus on issues of school restructuring, teacher quality, and educational equity. From 1994 to 2001, she served as executive director of the National Commission on Teaching and America's Future, a blue-ribbon panel whose 1996 report, *What Matters Most: Teaching for America's Future*, led to sweeping policy changes in teaching and teacher education. In 2006, the report was named one of the most influential affecting U.S. education, and Dr. Darling-Hammond was named one of the nation's 10 most influential people in educational policy over the last decade.

Among Dr. Darling-Hammond's more than 300 publications are *The Flat World and Education* (Teachers College Press, 2010); *Preparing Teachers for a Changing World: What Teachers Should Learn and Be Able to Do*, with John Bransford, for the National Academy of Education and winner of the Pomeroy Award from AACTE; *Teaching as the Learning Profession: A Handbook of Policy and Practice* (Jossey-Bass, 1999), coedited with Gary Sykes and winner of the National Staff Development Council's Outstanding Book Award for 2000; and *The Right to Learn: A Blueprint for Schools That Work*, recipient of the American Educational Research Association's Outstanding Book Award for 1998. Dr. Darling-Hammond received her doctorate in urban education from Temple University in 1978.

Robert Rothman is a senior fellow at the Alliance for Excellent Education. Previously, he was a senior editor at the Annenberg Institute for School Reform where he edited the Institute's quarterly magazine, *Voices* *in Urban Education.* He was also a study director at the National Research Council, where he led a committee on testing and assessment in the federal Title I program, which produced the report *Testing, Teaching and Learning* (edited with Richard F. Elmore) and a committee on teacher testing.

A nationally known education writer and editor, Mr. Rothman has also worked with Achieve and the National Center on Education and the Economy, and was a reporter and editor for *Education Week.* He has written numerous reports and articles on a wide range of education issues, and he is editor of *City Schools* (Harvard Education Press, 2007) and author of *Measuring Up: Standards, Assessments and School Reform* (Jossey-Bass, 1995), *Fewer, Clearer, Higher: How the Common Core State Standards Can Change Classroom Practice* (Harvard Education Press, 2013), and *Something in Common: The Common Core Standards and the Next Chapter in American Education* (Harvard Education Press, 2011). He has a degree in political science from Yale University.

Carol Campbell is associate professor of Leadership and Educational Change and director of the Knowledge Network for Applied Education Research (KNAER) at the Ontario Institute for Studies in Education, University of Toronto.

Previously, Dr. Campbell was executive director of the Stanford Center for Opportunity Policy in Education, Stanford University. From 2005 to 2010, Dr. Campbell held progressively senior positions in the Ontario Ministry of Education with a focus on the use of evidence to inform the Ontario education strategies. She was senior executive officer for the Literacy and Numeracy Secretariat, then appointed Ontario's first chief research officer for education, and became the founding director of the Education Research & Evaluation Strategy Branch. Dr. Campbell has worked as a policy and strategy advisor at school district and government levels in the United Kingdom and was a member of academic faculty at the Institute of Education, University of London. Originally from Scotland, she completed her doctorate at the University of Strathclyde.

Tan Lay Choo is chief executive of the Singapore Examinations and Assessment Board (SEAB). SEAB is a statutory board under the Singapore Ministry of Education, which is responsible for the design and development of national examinations and the promotion of the goals of Singapore's education system. The role of SEAB as an examining authority includes the organization and conduct of national examinations and the provision of advisory and consultancy services to the Ministry of Education and other government agencies. SEAB also conducts training for teachers and examination personnel on assessment theories and on the practice and management and conduct of examinations.

Ms. Tan has held several appointments in the Ministry of Education headquarters as well as in schools during her thirty years of service. She started her career as a mathematics teacher, served as a principal of a secondary school, and was subsequently appointed as a cluster superintendent overseeing a number of schools. Having served in several leadership appointments in headquarters, Ms. Tan had the opportunity to shape policies and design systemwide programs for a wide range of students, including gifted students, students with special needs, and low achievers. Ms. Tan also had a stint in manpower planning for the education system and contributed to policies on recruitment and career development of teachers.

Barry Pervin was assistant deputy minister of the Instruction and Leadership Development division at the Ontario Ministry of Education from 2007 to March 2014. In support of the ministry's overall agenda to improve student outcomes in Ontario schools, Mr. Pervin was responsible for policy and program development in areas such as teacher development, leadership development, safe and healthy schools, equity and inclusive education, and school board governance and labor relations.

During his years with the Ontario Public Service, he held positions in four different ministries including labor; skills development; training, colleges, and universities; and education. Mr. Pervin has played a leadership role in the Ontario Ministry of Education since 2001. He has an MA in public administration from Carleton University in Ottawa and an honors BA in sociology and education from Concordia University in Montreal.

Pasi Sahlberg is a visiting professor of practice at the Harvard University graduate school of education and the former director general of the Centre for International Mobility and Cooperation (CIMO) in Helsinki, Finland. He has global expertise in educational reforms, training teachers, coaching schools, and advising policymakers in more than 40 countries. Dr. Sahlberg has worked as a teacher, teacher-educator, senior advisor, and director, and served with the World Bank (in Washington, DC) and with the European Commission (in Torino, Italy) as education specialist. Dr. Sahlberg's latest book is titled *Finnish Lessons: What Can the World Learn About Educational Change in Finland?* (Teachers College Press, 2011), which won the Grawemeyer Award in 2013. He has a PhD from the University of Jyväskylä and is an adjunct professor at the Universities of Helsinki and Oulu.